Rudolf Steiner

Old and New Methods of Initiation

Fourteen Lectures given in Dornach,
Mannheim and Breslau
from
1 January to 19 March 1922

Translated by Johanna Collis

1991
Rudolf Steiner Press, London

Translated from the volume in the Complete Edition of Rudolf Steiner's works entitled *Alte und neue Einweihungsmethoden* (GA 210), first edition 1967.

Edited by Joan M. Thompson

The diagrams in the text were redrawn from Rudolf Steiner's blackboard sketches by Hedwig Frey.

Cover Design by Brian Gold

ISBN pb 0 85440 446 5
cloth 0 85440 456 2

Typeset by Emset, London NW10
Printed & Bound by Billings & Sons Ltd, Worcester.

CONTENTS

LECTURE ONE

Dornach, 1 January 1922

Yesterday[1] I spoke about initiation science. Today[2] I shall describe some aspects of what nowadays gives expression to initiation science. A profound breach now runs through the whole of civilization, a breach which brings much chaos to the world and which people who are fully aware cannot but experience with a sense of tragedy. One expression of this breach is the fact that human beings, when considering human dignity and their worth as human beings, can no longer find any connection with a world to which they look up—that world which gives the human soul religious feelings both profound and uplifting—namely, the world of moral values.

People look instead to the world of nature, to which, of course, they also belong. During the course of recent centuries the world of nature has come to appear before the human soul in such a way that it has absorbed the whole of reality, has absorbed every aspect of actual existence. The world of nature, with its laws which are indifferent to moral values, runs its course in accordance with external necessity, and in their everyday life human beings, too, are tied up in this necessity. However the bounds of this necessity are defined, if human beings feel themselves enclosed within such bounds, it is impossible for them to discover what it is that makes them human. Human beings have to look up from the world of nature to the world of moral values. We have to see the content of this moral world as something which ought to be, something which is the ideal. Yet no knowledge which is current today is capable of showing us how moral ideals can flow into the laws of nature and how necessity can be made to serve moral values.

We have to admit that today's world is divided into two parts which, for modern consciousness, are incompatible: the moral world and the material world. People see birth and death as the boundaries which encompass the only existence recognized by present-day knowledge. On the other hand they have to look up to a world which lies above birth and death, a world which is eternally meaningful, unlike the endlessly changing material world; and they have to think of their soul life as being linked with the eternal meaning of that world of moral values. The Platonic view of the world, containing as it did the last remnants of orientalism, saw the external world perceptible to the senses as a semblance, an illusion, and the world of ideas as the true, real world. But for modern human beings, if they remain within the confines of present-day consciousness, this Platonic world view has no answers.

But now initiation science wants to enter once again into human civilization and show us that behind the world perceived by our senses there stands a spiritual world, a mighty world, powerful and real, a world of moral values to which we may turn. It is the task of initiation science to take away from natural existence the absolute reality it assumes for itself and to give reality back once more to the world of moral values. It can only do so by using means of expression different from those given by today's language, today's world of ideas and concepts.

The language of initiation science still seems strange, even illusory, to people today because they have no inkling that real forces stand behind the expressions used, nor that, whatever kind of speech is used—whether ordinary everyday speech or speech formation—language cannot give full and adequate expression to what is seen and perceived. What, after all, do the words 'human being' signify, when only the speech sounds are considered, compared with the abundant richness of spirit, soul and body of an actual human being standing before us! In just such a way in initiation science a spiritual world—behind the world of the senses—living in the world of moral values, storms and flows, working in manifold ways. This initiation science has to select all manner of ways of expressing what, despite everything, will be far richer in its manifestation than any possible means of expression.

Today I should like to speak about certain expressions of this kind with regard to man's immediate existence, expressions which have been discussed here in one connection or another over the last few days and which are well known to those of you who have concerned yourselves over a period of time with anthroposophical spiritual science.

It is both right and wrong to say that the true being of man is beyond understanding. It is right in a certain sense, but not in the sense frequently meant nowadays. Yet the true being of man is indeed revealed to initiation science in a way which defies direct definitions, descriptions or explanations. To make use of a comparison I might say that defining the being of man is like trying to draw a picture of the fulcrum of a beam. It cannot be drawn. You can draw the left-hand and the right-hand portions of the beam but not the fulcrum upon which it turns. The fulcrum is the point at which the right-hand and the left-hand portions of the beam begin. In a similar way the profoundest element of the human being cannot be encompassed by adequate concepts and ideas. But it can be grasped by endeavouring to look at deviations from the true human being. The being of man represents the state of balance poised between deviations that constantly want to go off in opposite directions. Human beings throughout their life are permanently beset by two dangers: deviation in one of two directions, the luciferic or the ahrimanic.[3]

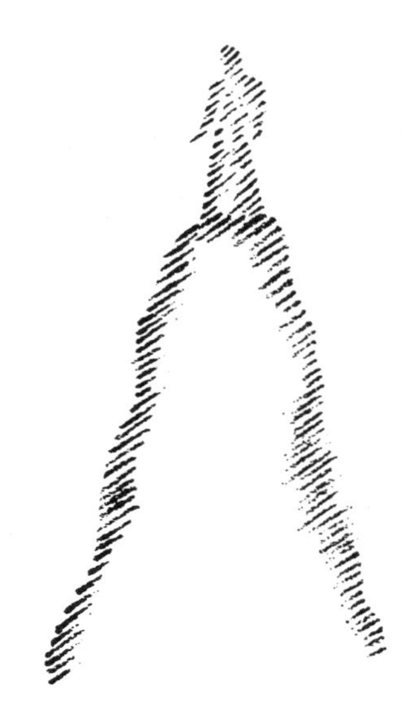

In ordinary life our state of balance is maintained because only a part of our total, our full being, is harnessed to our bodily form, and because it is not we who hold this bodily form in a state of balance within the world as a whole, but spiritual beings who stand behind us. Thus, in ordinary consciousness, we are on the whole unaware of the two dangers which can cause us to deviate from our state of balance towards one side or the other, towards the luciferic or the ahrimanic side. This is what is characteristic of initiation science. When we begin to comprehend the world in its true nature we feel as though we were standing on a high rock with one abyss on our right and another on our left. The abyss is ever-present, but in ordinary life we do not see this abyss, or rather these two abysses. To learn to know ourselves fully we have to perceive these abysses, or at least we have to learn about them. We are drawn in one direction towards Lucifer and in the other towards Ahriman. And the ahrimanic and the luciferic aspects can be characterized in relation to the body, the soul and the spirit.

Let us start from the point of view of man's physical being. This physical being, which the senses perceive as a unit, is in fact only seemingly so. Actually we are forever in tension between the forces which make us young and those which make us old, between the forces of birth and the forces of death. Not for a single moment throughout our life is only one of these forces present; always both are there.

When we are small, perhaps tiny, children, the youthful, luciferic forces predominate. But even then, deep down, are the ageing forces, the forces which eventually lead to the sclerosis of our body and, in the end, to death. It is necessary for both kinds of force to exist in the human body. Through the luciferic forces there is always a possibility of inclining towards, let me say, the phosphoric side, towards warmth. In the extreme situation of an illness this manifests in a fever, such as a pleuritic condition, a state of inflammation. This inclination towards fever and inflammation is ever-present and is only held in check or in balance by those other forces which want to lead towards solidified, sclerotic, mineral states. The nature of the human being arises from the state of balance between these two polar-opposite forces.

Valid sciences of human physiology and biology will only be possible when the whole human body and each of its separate organs, such as heart, lungs, liver, are seen to encompass polar opposites which incline them on the one hand towards dissolution into warmth and, on the other hand, towards consolidation into the mineral state. The way the organs function will only be properly understood once the whole human being, as well as each separate organ, are seen in this light. The science of human health and sickness will only find a footing on healthy ground once these polarities in the physical human being are able to be seen everywhere. Then it will be known, for instance, that at the change of teeth, around the seventh year, ahrimanic forces are setting to work in the head region; or that when the physical body starts to develop towards the warmth pole at puberty, this means that luciferic forces are at work; that in the rhythmical nature of the human being there are constant swings of the pendulum, physically too, between the luciferic and the ahrimanic aspect. Until we learn to speak thus, without any superstition, but with scientific exactness, about the luciferic and ahrimanic influences upon human nature—just as today we speak without superstition or mysticism about positive and negative magnetism, about positive and negative electricity, about light and darkness—we shall not be in a position to gain knowledge of the human being which can stand up to the abstract knowledge of inorganic nature that we have achieved during the course of recent centuries.

In an abstract way many people already speak about all kinds of polarities in the human being. Mystical, nebulous publications discuss all kinds of positive and negative influences in man. They shy away from ascending to a much more concrete, more spiritual, but spiritually entirely concrete plane, and so they speak in a manner about the human being's positive and negative polarities which is just as abstract as that in which they discuss polarities in inorganic nature. Real knowledge of the human being can only come about if we rise above the poverty-stricken concepts of positive and negative, the poverty-stricken concepts of polarity as found in inorganic nature, and ascend to the meaningful concepts of luciferic and ahrimanic influences in man.

Turning now to the soul element, in a higher sense the second element of man's being, we find the ahrimanic influence at work in everything that drives the soul towards purely intellectual rigid laws. Our natural science today is almost totally ahrimanic. As we develop towards ahrimanic soul elements, we discard anything that might fill our concepts and ideas with warmth. We submit only to whatever makes concepts and ideas ice-cold and dry as dust. So we feel especially satisfied in today's scientific thinking when we are ahrimanic, when we handle dry, cold concepts, when we can make every explanation of the world conform to the pattern we have established for inorganic, lifeless nature. Also, when we imbue our soul with moral issues, the ahrimanic influence is found in everything that tends towards what is pedantic, stiff, philistine on the one hand; but also in what tends towards freedom, towards independence, towards everything that strives to extract the fruits of material existence from this material existence and wants to become perfect by filling material existence.

Both ahrimanic and luciferic influences nearly always display two sides. In the ahrimanic direction, one of these—the pedantic, the philistine, the one-sidedly intellectual aspect—leads us astray. But on the other side there is also something that lies in mankind's necessary line of evolution, something which develops a will for freedom, a will to make use of material existence, to free the human being and so on.

The luciferic influence in the human soul is found in everything that makes us desire to fly upwards out of ourselves. This can create nebulous, mystical attitudes which lead us to regions where any thought of the material world seems ignoble and inferior. Thus we are led astray, misled into despising material existence entirely and into wanting instead to indulge in whatever lies above the material world, into wanting wings on which to soar above earthly existence, at least in our soul. This is how the luciferic aspect works on our soul. To the ahrimanic aspect of dull, dry, cold science is added a sultry mysticism of the kind that in religions leads to an ascetic disdain for the earth, and so on.

This description of the ahrimanic and luciferic aspects of soul life shows us that the human soul, too, has to find a balance between polar opposites. Like the ahrimanic, the luciferic aspect also reveals possibilities for deviation and, at the same time, possibilities for the necessary further evolution of the proper being of man. The deviation is a blurred, hazy, nebulous mysticism that allows any clear concepts to flutter away into an indeterminate, misty flickering of clarity and obscurity with the purpose of leading us up and away from ourselves. On the other hand, a luciferic influence which is entirely justifiable, and is indeed a part of mankind's necessary progress, is made manifest when we fill material existence with today's genuine life principles, not in order to make exhaustive use of the impulses of this material existence—as is the case with ahrimanic influences—but in order to paralyse material existence into becoming a semblance which can then be used in order to describe a supersensible realm, in order to describe something that is spiritually real, and yet—in this spiritual reality—cannot also be real in the world of the senses merely through natural existence.

Luciferic forces endow human beings with the possibility of expressing the spirit in the semblance of sense-perceptible existence. It is for this that all art and all beauty are striving. Lucifer is the guardian of beauty and art. So in seeking the right balance between luciferic and ahrimanic influences we may allow art—Lucifer—in the form of beauty, to work upon this balance. There is no question of saying that human beings must guard against ahrimanic and luciferic influences. What matters is for human beings to find the right attitude towards ahrimanic and luciferic influences, maintaining always a balance between the two. Provided this balance is maintained, luciferic influences may be permitted to shine into life in the form of beauty, in the form of art. Thus something unreal is brought into life as if by magic, something which has been transformed into a semblance of reality by the effort of human beings themselves.

It is the endeavour of luciferic forces to bring into present-day life something that has long been overtaken by world existence, something that the laws of existence cannot allow to be real in present-day life. If human beings follow a course of cosmic conservation, if they want to bring into the present certain forms of existence which were right and proper in earlier times, then they fall in the wrong way under the influence of the luciferic aspect. If, for instance, they bring in a view of the world that lives only in vague pictures such as were justifiable in ancient cosmic ages, if they allow everything living in their soul to become blurred and mingled, they are giving themselves up in the wrong way to luciferic existence. But if they give to external existence a form which expresses something it could not express by its own laws alone—marble can only express the laws of the mineral world—if they force marble to express something it would never be able to express by means of its own natural forces, the result is the art of sculpture; then, something which cannot be a reality in a sense-perceptible situation of this kind, something unreal, is brought as if by magic into real existence. This is what Lucifer is striving to achieve. He strives to lead human beings away from the reality in which they find themselves between birth and death into a reality which was indeed reality in earlier times but which cannot be genuine reality for the present day.

Now let us look at the spiritual aspect of the human being. We find that here, too, both luciferic and ahrimanic influences are called upon. In life here on earth the being of man expresses itself in the first instance in the alternating states of waking and sleeping. In the waking state the spiritual part of our being is fully given over to the material world. The following must be said in this connection: In sleep, from the moment of going to sleep to the moment of waking up, we find ourselves in a spirit-soul existence. On going to sleep we depart with our spirit-soul existence from our physical and etheric bodies, and on waking up we enter with our spirit and soul once again into our physical and etheric bodies. In sleep, you could say, we bear our state of soul-spirit within us; but on waking up we keep back our soul state almost entirely in the form of our soul life. Only with our spirit do we plunge fully into our body. So in the waking state in the present phase of human evolution we become with our spirit entirely body, we plunge into our body, at least to a very high degree. From the existence of our sleeping state we fall into that of our waking state. We are carried over from one state to the other. This is brought about by forces which we have to count among the ahrimanic forces.

Looking at the spiritual aspect of the human being, that is, at the alternation between waking and sleeping, which is what reveals our spiritual aspect in physical, earthly existence, we find that in waking up the ahrimanic element is most at work, while falling asleep is brought about chiefly by the luciferic element. From being entirely enveloped in our physical body, we are carried across into the free soul-spirit state. We are carried over into a state in which we no longer think in ahrimanic concepts but solely in pictures which dissolve sharp ahrimanic conceptual contours, allowing everything to interweave and become blurred. We are placed in a state in which to interweave in pictures is normal. In brief we can say: The ahrimanic element carries us, quite properly, from the sleeping to the waking state, and the luciferic element carries us, equally properly, from the waking state into the sleeping state.

Deviations occur when too little of the luciferic impulse is carried over into the waking state, making the ahrimanic impulse stronger than it should be in the waking state. If this happens, the ahrimanic impulse presses the human being down too strongly into his physical body, preventing him from remaining in the realm of the soul sentiments of good and evil, the realm of moral impulses. He is pushed down into the realm of emotions and passions. He is submerged in the life of animal instinct. His ego is made to enter too thoroughly into the bodily aspect.

Conversely, when the luciferic impulse works in an unjustified way in the human being it means that he carries too much of his waking life into his sleeping life. Dreams rise up in sleep which are too reminiscent of waking life. These work back into waking life and push it into an unhealthy kind of mysticism.

So you see, in every aspect of life a state of balance must be brought about in the human being by the two polarities, by the luciferic and the ahrimanic elements. Yet deviations can occur. As I have said, a proper physiology of the body, with a proper knowledge of health and sickness, will only be possible when we have learnt to find this polarity in every aspect of bodily life. Similarly, a valid psychology will only be possible when we are in a position to discover this polarity in the soul.

Nowadays, in the sciences that are regarded as psychology—the science of the soul—all sorts of chaotic things are said about thinking, feeling and willing. In the life of the soul thinking, feeling and willing also flow into one another. However pure our thoughts may be, as we link them together and take them apart we are using our will in our thoughts. And even in movements which are purely instinctive our thought impulses work into our will activity. Thinking, feeling and willing are nowhere separate in our soul life; everywhere they work into one another. If, as is the custom today, they are separated out, this is merely an abstract separation; to speak of thinking, feeling and willing is then merely to speak of three abstractions. Certainly we can distinguish between what we call thinking, feeling and willing, and as abstract concepts they may help us to build up our knowledge of what each one is; but this by no means gives us a true picture of reality.

We gain a true picture of reality only if we see feeling and willing in every thought, thinking and willing in every feeling and thinking and feeling in every act of will. In order to see—in place of that abstract thinking, feeling and willing—our concrete living and surging soul life, we must also picture to ourselves how our soul life is deflected to one polarity or the other—for instance, how it is deflected to the ahrimanic polarity and there lives in thoughts. However many will impulses there may be in these thoughts, if we learn to recognize, at a higher level of knowledge, the special characteristics of the ahrimanic element, then we can feel the polarity of thinking in the soul. And if we see the soul deflected in the other direction, towards the will, then—however much thought content there may be in this will activity—if we have grasped the luciferic nature of the will, we shall have understood the living nature of the will in our soul life. All abstractions, concepts, ideas in us must be transformed into living vision. This we will not achieve unless we resolve to ascend to a view of the luciferic and the ahrimanic elements.

As regards the life of mankind through history, too, the pictures we form are only real if we are capable of perceiving the working and surging of the luciferic and ahrimanic elements in the different periods of history. Let us look, for instance, at the period of history which starts with Augustine[4] and reaches to the end of the Middle Ages and the beginning of modern times, the fifteenth century. Let us look at this period and see how in external life people preferred to allow impulses to work which came from their deepest inner being, out of their emotional life; let us see how people during this period wanted to shape even the external life of society and the state in accordance with what they believed they could discern of the divine impulses within themselves. We feel quite clearly that the luciferic impulse was at work in this period of history.

Now go to more recent times and see how people turn and look outwards towards the mechanical and physical aspects of the world which can only be adequately comprehended in the right way by thinking and by contact with the external world. It is obvious that the ahrimanic element is at work in this period. Yet this must not tempt us to declare the period from Augustine to Galileo to be luciferic and the period from Galileo to the present time to be ahrimanic. This would in turn be an ahrimanic judgement, an intellectualistic interpretation. If we want to make the transition from an intellectualistic to a living interpretation, to a recognition of life as an experience in which we share, of which we are a part, then we shall have to express ourselves differently. We shall have to say: During the period from Augustine to Galileo, human beings had to resist the luciferic element in their striving for balance. And in more recent times human beings have to resist the ahrimanic element in their striving for balance.

We must understand ever more clearly that in our civilization as it progresses it is not a matter of whether we say one thing or another. What matters is being able to decide, in a given situation, whether one thing or another can be said. However true it may be to say, in an abstract way, that the Middle Ages were luciferic and more recent times ahrimanic, what matters is that this abstract truth bears no real impulse. The real impulse comes into play when we say: In the Middle Ages human beings maintained their uprightness by combating the luciferic element; in modern times they maintain their uprightness by combating the ahrimanic element. In an external, abstract sense something that is in reality no more than an empty phrase can be perfectly true. But as regards the particular situation of human existence in question, a thing that is real in our life of ideas can only be something that is actually inwardly present. What people today must avoid more than anything else is to fall into empty phrases. Again and again we come across situations in which people who believe themselves to be standing in anthroposophical life say: So-and-so said something which was in perfect agreement with Anthroposophy. We are not concerned with an outward agreement in words alone. What matters is the spirit, the living spirit, the living reality within which something stands. If we concern ourselves solely with the external, logical content of what people say today, we do not avoid the danger of the empty phrase.

In one circle or another recently I have a number of times given a striking example of how strangely certain statements, which are perfectly correct in themselves, appear when illuminated by a sense for reality. In 1884, in the German Reichstag, Bismarck made a remarkable statement when he felt threatened by the approach of social democracy.[5] He wanted to dissuade the majority of the working population from following their radical social-democratic leaders, and this is what spurred him to say: Every individual has the right to work; grant to every individual the right to work, let the state find work for everybody, provide everybody with what they need in order to live—thus spoke the German Chancellor—when they are old and can no longer work, or when they are ill, and you will see that the broad masses of the workers will turn tail on the promises of their leaders. This is what Prince Bismarck said in the German Reichstag in 1884.

Curiously enough, if you go back almost a hundred years you find that another political figure said the same, almost verbatim: It is our human duty to grant every individual the right to work, to let the state find work for all, so long as they can work, and for the state to care for them when they are ill and can no longer work. In 1793 Robespierre[6] wanted to incorporate this sentence in the democratic constitution. Is it not remarkable that in 1793 the revolutionary Robespierre and in 1884 Prince Bismarck—who certainly had no wish to be another Robespierre—said exactly the same thing. Two people can say exactly the same, yet it is not the same. Curiously, too, Bismarck referred in 1884 to the fact that every worker in the state of Prussia was guaranteed the right to work, since this was laid down in the Prussian constitution of 1794. So Bismarck not only says the same, but he says that what Robespierre demanded was laid down in the Prussian constitution. The real situation, however, was as follows: Bismarck only spoke those words because he felt the approach of a threat which arose from the very fact that what stood word for word in the Prussian constitution was actually not the case at all.

I quote this example not because it is political but because it is a striking demonstration of how two people can say the same thing, word for word, even though the reality in each case is the opposite. Thus I want to make you aware that it is time for us to enter upon an age when what matters, rather than the actual words, is our experience of reality. If we fail in this, then in the realm of spiritual life we shall fall into empty phrases which play such a major role in the spiritual life of today. And this transition from mere correctness of content to truth livingly experienced is to be brought about through the entry of initiation science into human civilization, initiation science which progresses from mere logical content to the experience of the spiritual world. Those who view correctly the external symptoms of historical development in the present and on into the near future will succeed, out of these symptoms, in achieving a feeling, a sense, for the justified and necessary entry of initiation science into world civilization. This is what I wanted to place before your souls today by way of a New Year's contemplation.

LECTURE TWO

Dornach, 7 January 1922

Today I shall add to what has been said over the past few days, both before and after Christmas, about the Being of Christ. Our angle of approach to the question of Christ will be to relate it in a brief sketch chiefly to the world-wide social question. Mankind has at the present time an urgent need to reach a global understanding. Yet whatever sphere of life we turn to, we find precious little of any such understanding. The need for an understanding is there. What is not there is any talent on the part of human beings to come to such an understanding. We see how attempts are made to consult one another about important aspects of life. We see congresses taking place everywhere. With regard to the matters being discussed at these congresses, what is to be found in the depths of human souls is quite different from the words which are exchanged there. In the words exchanged at these congresses there are appearances which are deceptive. These appearances are supposed to give the impression that individual human beings everywhere desire to come to terms with one another, or something similar. But such coming to terms cannot be achieved anywhere, because it is not actually individual human beings who are speaking with one another but members of various nations. Only the external appearance makes it seem as though individuals were speaking with one another. What is actually speaking through each one are the very varied beings of the different nations. And since it is in the very nature of human beings these days to notice only the verbal content of words and not the source of the words—not the soil in which they are rooted—since human beings fail to discern these fundamental aspects of life, it is simply not noticed that it is the folk daemons who are speaking with one another, rather than human being with human being.

We would be hard put to it to find clearer proof of the fact that Christianity is today not realized in the world. Christianity is not realized, for fully to understand Christ means: to find man as man within oneself. Christ is no folk god, no god of any race. Christ is not the god of any group of human beings. He is the god of the individual, in so far as the individual is a member of the human race as a whole. Only when we can understand the Christ-being, through all the means available to us, as the God of mankind, only then will Christ come to have what will certainly be the greatest possible social significance for the globe as a whole.

We have to understand very clearly that there are things which hold sway in the depths of the soul, things which do not find their way into those words that remain stuck in empty phrases as a result of the differences between the folk daemons. Out of the situation in which people are content to reside at present, it is not possible to bring about what can actually only be brought about today out of the profound depths of man's being. Today what is needed is profundity, a willingness to enter into the profound depths of man's being, if forces of advance, forces of fruitful progress are to enter into earth evolution. What can be heard today in every corner of the earth does not to any extent even touch the surface of all that is rooted in the human being. What ought now to enter into mankind is the quest for what is most profoundly rooted in the being of man.

Let us now show in a few simple outlines the main differences that exist in people's attitudes to what could lead to a recognition and an understanding of the question of Christ. I have often drawn the distinction for you between people of the West, people of the East, and people of the middle region between West and East. This distinction can be viewed from very varied standpoints. Justice can only be done to it if it is considered without any kind of prejudice and with the utmost impartiality, if we refrain from looking with sympathy or antipathy at one or other of these divisions, perhaps because we happen to belong to one or the other of them ourselves. Today all the people of the world must work together in order to bring forth true unity in Christ. It can certainly be said that in the most varied parts of the world, in the very depths of mankind, the impulse exists towards finding this unity. But the search must take us into the profound depths.

Turning first to what appears now in the civilizations of the West, we discover that the essential element in these western civilizations finds an expression in the type of spirituality which is valid today. This special spirituality of today has the characteristic of taking the form of abstractness; it celebrates its greatest triumphs in ideas and abstractions. These ideas, these abstractions, are most suited to gaining a knowledge of nature as it appears to our senses, and a knowledge of that aspect of social life which has to take place as a result of the forces of the sense-perceptible world. With these forces, which I shall call the western forces, it is quite possible to penetrate into the depths of the human being and of the universe. Above all, these forces of the West have provided the foundation for scientific thinking and have sought those impulses of social life which derive from scientific thinking and which mankind will need in the future in order to shape life on earth in a possible way. What follows will show this to be so. By no means all the treasures of western spiritual life have been brought to the surface.

To start with, it is perfectly true that today's natural science could only be founded on those fundamental forces of man's being which can be most adequately expressed in the spirituality of abstractness and ideas. But it is also true that in everything that has been revealed there is another essential element as well. What has been revealed in the thought processes of natural science, and the social thought processes that go with it, can indeed be taken right up to the spiritual realm. A progression can be made from the laws of nature to a recognition of the spiritual beings within nature. These beings of nature are divine and spiritual. And if Christianity is to be understood in a way that befits mankind's most current needs, it will have to be permeated with that very spirit which has so far only poured itself out into natural science and its social consequences through the forces of the West. Any world conception gained out of these forces of the West can only be satisfying if it can be expressed in clearly defined, sharply contoured concepts and ideas. Human beings will need such clear, sharply defined concepts for the future of the earth. They will have to learn to present the highest spiritual content to mankind in terms which are every bit as clearly defined as are the natural and social concepts arising out of the forces of the West.

Let us turn now to the forces of the East. Here, what is made clearest to us is the following: If, out of the forces of the East, we want to attempt to describe Christianity, or indeed anything divine and spiritual, in sharp, clearly-defined terms, our efforts will be in vain. Starting with Russia and going eastwards through Asia, the whole of the East brings forth forces in its peoples which are not capable of rising up to spiritual, divine realms in sharply defined concepts. The forces here are suitable for rising up to the spirit out of the depths of feeling.

In order to describe Christianity in a manner befitting the West we need philosophy, we need a concept of the world which is clothed in modern thought forms. But to describe Christianity with the forces of the East we cannot find such thought forms if we remain at the level of outer nationality. If we remain in the external, sense-perceptible world we have to grasp other means. For instance, we have to describe the feelings which are found as soon as we start going further and further eastwards, even in the regions of central Europe bordering on the East. Look at the living rooms of simple people and see the altar with the Mother of God in the corner. See how the image of the Mother of God is greeted by visitors as they arrive. Everywhere the first greeting is for the Mother of God, and only then are greetings exchanged with the people in the room. This is something that emanates from all the forces of the human being, with the exception of those of abstract ideas. There exists a radical contrast between West and East in the inmost feelings for what is divine and spiritual. Yet all these forces are root forces which can develop further, which can put forth leaves and shoots and finally bear fruit, if only they can come to a fundamental understanding of themselves.

The West is capable of reaching a conception and a feeling of the Father God in a manner which befits the new human spirit, a conception and a feeling beside which those other divine spiritual beings, the Son and the Spirit, can stand. But above all it is the task of the West to contribute to the world concepts and feelings about the Father God which are different from those possible in earlier times, when only vague presentiments could be achieved in this respect. On the other hand, if the forces mainly present in the East are developed—the forces which can only be described suitably in what might be called a non-intellectual way with the help of external gestures—if these forces are developed with the feelings and will impulses they entail, and if they take up also the forces streaming towards them from the West, they will be able to come to a fitting concept and a fitting feeling of the Son God. In this way mankind's development into the future can only be rightly understood when the things that are achieved in the different regions of the earth are taken to be contributions to a total outcome.

Especially the more outstanding spirits in the West—though mostly they are not aware of this themselves—may be seen to be struggling for a concept of the Father God, a concept arising from the foundations of natural science. And in the East we see in the external gestures of the people, in what comes out of their feelings and their will, how they are wrestling for an understanding of the Son God, the Christ. The middle region stands between these two extremes. This is shown clearly by what has been developing more recently in the culture of the middle region. It is characteristic of modern theology in Central Europe that it is uncertain in its understanding of the Father and also in its understanding of the Son, the Christ. Endeavours to find such an understanding are taken immensely earnestly. But this very earnestness has caused the endeavours to be split in two separate directions. On the one hand we see knowledge developing, and on the other we see faith. We see how knowledge is to contain only what applies to the sense-perceptible world and everything that belongs to it. And we see how faith, which must not be allowed to become knowledge, is allotted everything that makes up man's relationship to what is divine and spiritual. These divergent endeavours express the quest, a quest which cannot achieve an adequate concept and feeling for either the Father God or the Son God without joining forces with the other regions of the earth, with East and West.

How such a global working together in the spirit should take place can be seen especially in the beginnings made by the Russian philosopher Vladimir Soloviev.[1] This Russian philosopher has taken western thought forms into his own thinking. If you are thoroughly familiar with the thought forms of the West, you will find them everywhere in Soloviev's work. But you will find that they are handled differently from the way in which they are handled in the West. If you approach Soloviev with a thinking prepared in the West you will have to relearn something—not about the content of thoughts, but about the attitude of the human being towards the content of thoughts. You will have to undergo a complete inner metamorphosis.

Take what I regard as one of the cardinal passages in Soloviev's work, a passage he has invested with a great deal of human striving towards a knowledge of man's being and his relationship with the world. He says: Human beings must strive for perfection. This endeavour is expressed in the way they strive for the truth. By uniting truth ever more and more closely with their souls they will become ever more and more perfect. Without this movement towards perfection human life would be worthless. Human beings must have the prospect of reaching the highest pinnacles of perfection through truth, as otherwise their lives would be null and void. At the same time they must have a part in immortality, for a striving for perfection destined only to be forfeited in death would be a fraud of universal proportions.

This is expressed by Soloviev in words and thought forms which imitate those of the West, or rather the thought forms are borrowed and the word forms imitated. But the *way* in which it is expressed, and the way the impulse to express it is present—this is impossible in the West. You will not find it expressed in this way by any western philosopher. Just imagine Mill or Bergson saying such a thing! It is unimaginable. These are the things for which we must develop a sense nowadays. We must develop a sense for the living sources from which words flow. The content of words is growing ever more insignificant in comparison with world concepts. A sense for the living source of things is what has real significance.

We can today only imagine a person to be capable of speaking in the way Soloviev does if he still has a true experience of what every one of his compatriots does before the icon of the Mother of God. Such a person must stand immersed in his people, a people capable of bringing proof without having to base it on abstract, logical foundations, a people for whom proofs based on mere abstract logic are less important than those which come out of the whole human being.

We feel in these words of Soloviev how, coming from the East, what is said comes out of the total being of man, not just out of mere intellectual human understanding. Because Soloviev speaks and thinks and feels out of the very foundations of his people, the whole of his world conception tends in the direction of the Christ. Because he has also taken on, as something from outside, the thought forms of the West, his world conception at the same time tends in the direction of the Father God as well as the Christ. Thus we discover in him something which it is almost impossible to find anywhere in the present, and that is a fundamental, clear distinction in the feelings of a human being between the way to the Father God and the way to Christ, the Son God. In a spirit such as Vladimir Soloviev we find a hint of what must come about in the future. For what must come about is a working together of the different regions of the earth, and this cannot come about if any one region imagines itself to be in possession of the whole.

Mankind came forth out of a unity. If we go back into the obscure, remote antiquity of human evolution we come to an archetypal wisdom which was still instinctive and which, because of this, still filled the whole human being. Throughout the whole of the earth people communicated with one another, not yet by means of the logical content of language but externally, by means of the then still existing inner capacity to communicate in gestures, of which today we no longer have the faintest idea. People communicated with one another by means of something which today, if at all, remains only in those remnants of the treasure-house of language which we call interjections. Naturally, if you exclaim: Whew! or sigh: Oh! you will be understood the world over. This kind of understanding resembles the communication that took place at the time of instinctive archetypal wisdom. Today we no longer know how to feel in language as a whole what the archetypal wisdom felt in it. All that remains for us is our feeling for the interjections which, of course, we only use occasionally.

In parenthesis let me add that it is quite in keeping that, out of people's dissatisfaction arising from the whole chaos of our spiritual life, authors are starting to write novels in interjections. This does happen nowadays. I am not quoting, but simply mention that you can find prose passages today which read: Ah! Oh! Wow! Eh! Then the writer begins: Once there was—and then come more interjections. Some recent novels are tending in this direction. As symptoms they are not without significance. As I said, this just in passing.

We have lost the ability to invest the whole of language with what we today only invest in interjections. Consider the following: 'Anthropos' means man, human being. 'Anthropoid' means man-like, that is, the higher animals. The final syllable, 'oid', is connected with the word which means 'like, similar to'. Now there is a remarkable connection between Greek and, for instance, German. In German the final syllable meaning 'like' is 'ig'. This is pronounced 'ich'. If we speak this final syllable by itself, 'ich', we have the German word for ego, for our own being. This is one kind of etymological truth. The 'ich' in the human being is what strives in its totality to become like the universe. 'Ich' is like, is similar to, everything; microcosm compared with macrocosm. Of course to go into things in this way cannot be done in the superficial manner in which etymology and linguistics are conducted nowadays. One has to go down to a more profound level and gain a sense for the way in which the sounds are connected with one another.

I brought this up merely to show one of the facets of what we must do to enter into language in search of a far more alive content than exists nowadays in the languages of the world. We must strive not to take words merely as words but to seek out their living roots. We must learn to understand that two people can say the same thing and yet mean something quite different, depending on the way of life from which it stems. We shall need such a deepening of our feelings in order to enter into the kind of global working together which will be necessary if mankind is to set out once more on the upward path.

It is not enough to address Christ as: Lord, Lord! Christ must become something which fills the whole human being. This can only happen if we support our understanding with something which comes to meet us when we look towards the archetypal wisdom of the world and remind ourselves that that wisdom made mankind into a totality. It was, though, a totality in which all individuality was lost. But evolution progressed. Human beings became ever more individualized. They felt more and more that they were approaching the point at which each one feels separated from all the others, for that alone guarantees the experience of freedom. So something had to be poured out into human evolution which might once more bring unity to the whole earth. This was the Christ-being. The Christ-being will only be fully understood when we gain from it a feeling for the impulse to bring about a social unity of human beings over the whole earth. Or looked at the other way round: Only the Christ-being, fully understood, can lead to a right social impulse throughout the world.

We look to the archetypal wisdom, which developed out of instinctive foundations to a certain high degree of vision—not our vision but an ancient vision. We find this vision in its final phase expressed in the archetypal symbol of what the three wise men, the three Magi from the East, brought to Christ Jesus. What led them to Christ Jesus was the most ancient and, at that time, the highest wisdom of mankind. And at the same time we are told by another evangelist how the individual human being, out of the inmost forces of his soul, as though in a dream—for the individual is alone when he dreams, even though he may be in company with others—is also led to Christ Jesus, how the shepherds in the field, dreaming in their solitary souls, are led to Chist Jesus: the first beginning of a new age. By the fourth century AD mankind had lost the wisdom of the Magi from the East. At the time of the Mystery of Golgotha the highest archetypal wisdom—about to fade—meets and mingles with something that appears at first utterly devoid of wisdom, something which must be developed ever further, until in the end it can take root in every individual human being, uniting all mankind.

In his youth, Augustine[2] endeavoured to save the last remnants of the wisdom brought to Christ Jesus by the Magi from the East. But Augustine had already received it in a form to which he could not confess in the long run. It was even then too degenerate. So he had to turn to what had been present at the beginning of evolution, to what will have to progress ever further and further, to what must be sought in order that mankind may once again find unity over the whole face of the earth.

If we pursue these hints—for that is all they are for the moment—in the right way, they will give us forces which will lead ever more profoundly into an understanding of the Christ-being, to an understanding of the Mystery of Golgotha. This is what I wanted to add to what we have been saying about the Being of Christ.

LECTURE THREE

Dornach, 8 January 1922

Today we shall consider the differentiations in mankind from another viewpoint, namely that of history. With the express aim of promoting an understanding for the present time we shall look at human evolution starting at a point immediately following the catastrophe of Atlantis. If human evolution can be considered to encompass any evolution of civilization, then we shall find the first decisive period of development to be the culture epoch of ancient India. In my book *Occult Science*[1] you will find this culture of ancient India described from a particular viewpoint. Though the Vedas and Indian philosophy are rightly admired, they are actually only echos of that ancient culture, of which there exist no written records. In the words of today we have to describe the culture of ancient India as a religious culture in the highest sense. To understand this properly we shall have to discuss it more thoroughly.

The religious element of ancient Indian culture included what we today would call science and art. The total spiritual life of the whole human being was encompassed by this culture for which the most pertinent description is that it was a religious culture. This religious culture generates the feeling in human beings that in the depths of their being they are linked with a divine, spiritual world. This feeling was developed so intensely that the whole of life was illumined by it. Their clearer states of consciousness, which were preparations for today's waking state, and also their dream consciousness, which became lost in our chaotic dream and sleep life as evolution progressed, were both states of consciousness filled with an instinctive awareness of the links between the human realm and the divine, spiritual realm.

But our idea of religion today is of something rather general. The concept of religion makes us think too strongly of something general, something abstract and rather detached from everyday life. For the people about whom we are speaking, however, religion and the content they associated with it gave them a knowledge expressed in pictures, a knowledge of the being of man and an extensive picture knowledge of the structure of the universe.

We have to imagine, though, that what lived in these people's view of the world, by way of a picture knowledge of the structure of the universe, in no way resembled our modern knowledge of astronomy or astrophysics. Our astronomy and astrophysics show us the mechanics of the universe. The ancient Indian people had a universe of picture images populated with divine, spiritual beings. There was as yet no question, in the present sense, of any external, merely mechanical rules governing the relationships between heavenly bodies or their relative movements. When those people looked up to the starry heavens they saw in the external constellations and movements of the stars only something perfectly familiar to them in their picture consciousness. It was something which may be described as follows.

Suppose we were to see a vivid, lively scene with bustling crowds and people going about all kinds of business, perhaps a public festival with much going on. Then we go home, and next morning the newspaper carries a report about the festival we ourselves attended. Our eyes fall on the dead letters of the printed page. We know what they mean and when we read the words they give us a weak, pale idea of all the lively bustle we experienced the day before. This can be compared with what the ancient Indian people saw in their instinctive vision and in relation to this what they saw in the constellations and movements of the stars. The constellations and movements of the stars were no more than written characters, indeed pale written characters. If they had copied down these characters on paper, they would have felt them to be no more than a written description of reality.

What these people saw behind the written characters was something which they not only came to know with their understanding but also to love with their feelings. They were unable merely to take into their ideas all that they grasped in pictures about the universe; they also developed lively feelings for these things. At the same time they developed a permanent feeling that whatever they did, even the most complicated actions, was an expression of the cosmos filled with divine spiritual weaving. They felt their limbs to be filled with this divine, spiritual cosmic weaving. They felt their understanding to be filled with this divine spiritual weaving, and likewise their courage and their will. Thus, speaking of their own deeds, they were able to say: Divine, spiritual beings are doing this. And since in those ancient times people knew very well that Lucifer and Ahriman are also to be found among those divine, spiritual beings, so were they aware that because divine, spiritual beings worked in them, they were therefore capable of committing evil as well as good deeds.

With this description I want to call up in you an idea of what this religion was like. It filled the whole human being, it brought the whole human being into a relationship with the abundance of the cosmos. It was cosmic wisdom and at the same time it was a wisdom which revealed man. But then progress in human evolution first caused the most intense religious feelings to pale. Of course, religion remained, in all later ages, but the intensity of religious life as it was in this first Indian age paled. First of all what paled was the feeling of standing within the realm of divine, spiritual beings with one's deeds and will impulses. In the ancient Persian age, the second post-Atlantean cultural epoch, people still had this feeling to some extent, but it had paled. In the first post-Atlantean epoch this feeling was a matter of course. In the second cultural blossoming, the ancient Persian time, the profoundest, most intense religious feelings paled, so human beings had to start developing something out of themselves in order to maintain their link with the cosmic, divine spiritual realm in a more active manner than had at first been the case. So we might say: The first post-Atlantean period was the most intensely religious of all. And in the second period religion faded somewhat, but human beings had to develop something by inner activity, something which would unite them once more with the cosmic beings of spirit and soul.

Of all the words we know, there is one we could use to describe this, although it was coined in a later age. It comes from an age which still possessed an awareness of what had once been a part of human evolution in ancient times. When an ancient Indian looked up to the heavens, he sensed the presence of individual beings everywhere, one divine spiritual being next to another—a whole population of divine spiritual beings. But this faded, so that what had been individualized, what had been individual, divine, spiritual beings faded into a general, homogeneous spiritual cosmos. Think of the following picture: Imagine a swarm of birds close by. You see each individual bird, but as the swarm flies further and further away it becomes a black blur, a homogeneous shape. In the same way the divine spiritual cosmos became a blurred image when human beings moved spiritually away from it.

The ancient Greeks still had an inkling of the fact that once, in the distant past, something like this had been at the foundation of what human beings saw in the spiritual world. Therefore they took into their language the word 'sophia'. A divine, spiritual cosmos had once, as a matter of course, poured itself into human beings and had taken human beings into itself. But now man had to approach what he saw from a spiritual distance—a homogeneous cosmos—by his own inner activity. This the Greeks, who still had a feeling for these things, called by the expression: 'I love'; that is: 'philo'. So we can say that in the second post-Atlantean period, that of ancient Persia, the initiates had a twofold religion where earlier on religion had been onefold. Now they had philosophy and religion. Philosophy had been achieved. Religion had come down from the more ancient past, but it had paled.

Passing now to the third post-Atlantean period, we reach a further paling of religion. But we also come to a paling of philosophy. The actual, concrete process that took place must be imagined as follows. In ancient Persian times there existed this homogeneous shape made up of cosmic beings and this was felt to be the light that flooded through the universe, the primeval light, the primeval aura, Ahura Mazda. But now people retreated even further from this vision and began in a certain way to pay more attention to the movements of the stars and of the starry constellations. They now sensed less in regard to the divine, spiritual beings who existed in the background and more in regard to the written characters. From this arose something which we find in two different forms in the Chaldean wisdom and the Egyptian wisdom, something which comprised knowledge about the constellations and the movements of the stars. At the same time, the inner activity of human beings had become even more important. They not only had to unite their love with this divine Sophia who shone through the universe as the primeval light, but they had to unite their own destiny, their own position in the world, with what they saw within the universe in a cosmic script provided by the starry constellations and the starry movements. Their new achievement was thus a Cosmo-Sophia. This cosmosophy still contained an indication of the divine, spiritual beings, but what was seen tended to be merely a cosmic script expressing the deeds of these beings. Beside this there still existed philosophy and religion, which had both faded.

In order to understand this we must realize that what we today call philosophy is naturally only an extremely weak, pale shadow image of what was still felt to be more alive in the Mysteries of the third post-Atlantean period and what in an even paler form the Greeks later called philosophy. In the culture of the third post-Atlantean period we see everywhere expressions of these three aspects of the human spirit: a cosmosophy, a philosophy and a religion.[2] And we only gain proper pictures of these when we know we have to remind ourselves that right up to this time human beings lived in their soul life more outside the earthly realm than within it. Looking for instance at the Egyptian culture from this point of view—and it was even more pronounced in the Chaldean—we see it rightly only if we remind ourselves that those who had any part in this culture indeed took the most intimate interest in the constellations of the stars as evening approached. For example they awaited certain manifestations from Sirius, they observed the planetary constellations and applied what they saw there to the way the Nile gave them what they needed for their earthly life. But they did not speak in the first instance of the earthly realm. This earthly realm was one field of their work, but when they spoke of the field they were tilling they did so in a way which related it to the extraterrestrial realm. And they named the varying appearances of the patch of earth they inhabited in accordance with whatever the stars revealed as the seasons followed one upon another. They judged the earth in accordance with the heavens. From the soul point of view, daytime brought them darkness. Light came into this darkness when they could interpret what the day brought in terms of what the starry heavens of the night showed them.

What people in those times saw might be expressed thus: The face of the earth is dark when the sun obscures my vision with dazzling brightness; but light falls on the field of my daily work when my soul shines upon it through starry wisdom.

Writing down a sentence like this gives us a sense for what the realm of feeling in this third post-Atlantean period was like. From this in turn we sense how those who still stood in the after-echoes of such a realm of feeling could say to the Greeks, to those who belonged to the fourth post-Atlantean cultural period: Your view of the world, indeed your whole life, is childlike, for you have knowledge only of the earth. Your ancestors in ancient times knew how to illumine the earth with the light of the heavens, but you live in the darkness of earth.

The ancient Greeks experienced this darkness of earth as something light. Their inclination was gradually to overcome and transform the older cosmosophy. So, as everything that looked down from the broad heavens became paler still, they transformed the older cosmosophy into a geosophy. Cosmosophy was nothing more than a tradition for them, something they could learn about when they looked back to those who had passed it down to them from earlier times.

Pythagoras, for instance, stood at the threshold of the fourth post-Atlantean period when he journeyed to the Egyptians, to the Chaldeans and even further into Asia in order to gather whatever those who lived there could give him of the wisdom of their forefathers in the Mysteries, whatever they could give him of what had been their cosmosophy, their philosophy and their religion. And what was still comprehensible for him was then just that: cosmosophy, philosophy, religion.

However, there is something we today take far too little into consideration: This geosophy of the ancient Greeks was a knowledge, a wisdom which, in relation to the earthly world, gave human beings a feeling of being truly connected with the earth, and this connection with the earth was something which had a quality of soul. The connection with the earth of a cultured Greek had a quality of soul. It was characteristic for the Greeks to populate springs with nymphs, to populate Olympus with gods. All this points, not to a geology, which envelops the earth in nothing but concepts, but to a geosophy in which spiritual beings are livingly recognized and knowingly experienced. This is something which mankind today knows only in the abstract. Yet right into the fourth century AD it was still something that was filled with life.

Right into the fourth century AD a geosophy of this kind still existed. And something of this geosophy, too, came to be preserved in tradition. For instance we can only understand what we find in the work of Scotus Erigena,[3] who brought over from the island of Ireland what he later expressed in his *De divisione naturae*, if we take it as a tradition arising out of a geosophical view. For in the fifth post-Atlantean period, which was in preparation then and which began in the fifteenth century, geosophy, too, paled. There then began the era in which human beings lost their inner connection with, and experience of, the universe. Geosophy is transformed, we might say, into geology. This is meant in the widest possible sense and comprises not only what today's academic philosophy means by the term. Cosmosophy was transformed into cosmology. Philosophy was retained but given an abstract nature—which in reality ought to be called philology, had this term not already been taken to denote something even more atrocious than anything one might like to include in philosophy.

There remains religion, which is now totally removed from any real knowledge and basically assumed by people to be nothing more than tradition. People of a nature capable of being creatively religious are no longer a feature of civilized life in general in this fifth post-Atlantean period. Look at those who have come and gone. None have been creatively religious in the true sense of the word. And this is only right and proper. In the preceding epochs, in the first, second, third and fourth post-Atlantean periods, there were always those who were creatively religious, personalities who were creative in the realm of religion, for it was always possible to bring down something from the cosmos, or at least to bring something up out of the realm of the earth. So in the Greek Mysteries—those called the Chthonian Mysteries in contrast to the heavenly Mysteries—which brought up their inspiration out of the depths of the earth in various ways—in these Mysteries geosophy was chiefly brought into being.

By entering into the fifth post-Atlantean period and standing fully within it, human beings were thrown back upon themselves. They now made manifest what came out of themselves, '-logy', the lore, the knowledge out of themselves. Thus knowledge of the universe becomes a world of abstractions, of logical concepts, of abstract ideas. Human beings have lived in this world of abstract ideas since the fifteenth century. And with this world of abstract ideas, which they summarize in the laws of nature, they now seek to grasp out of themselves what was revealed to human beings of earlier times. It is quite justified that this age no longer brings forth any religiously creative natures, for the Mystery of Golgotha falls in the fourth post-Atlantean period, and this Mystery of Golgotha is the final synthesis of religious life. It leads to a religion that ought to be the conclusion of earthly religious streams and strivings. With regard to religion, all subsequent ages can really only point back to this Mystery of Golgotha.

So the statement, that since the beginning of the fifth post-Atlantean period it is no longer possible for religiously productive individuals to appear, is not a criticism or a reprimand aimed at historical development. It is a statement of something positive because it can be justified by the occurrence of the Mystery of Golgotha.

In this way we conjure up before our eyes the course of human evolution with regard to spiritual streams and spiritual endeavours. In this way we can see how it has come about that we stand today in the midst of something that is, basically, no longer connected with the world about us but has come out of the human being, something in which the human being is productive and must become ever more productive. By further developing all these abstract things human beings will ascend once more through Imaginations to a kind of geosophy and cosmosophy. Through Inspiration they will deepen cosmosophy and ascend to a true philosophy, and through Intuition they will deepen philosophy until they can move towards a truly religious view of the world which will once more be able to unite with knowledge.

It is necessary to say that today we are only in the very first, most elementary beginnings of this progress. Since the final third of the nineteenth century there has shone into the earthly world from the spiritual world something which we can take to be a giving-back of spiritual revelations. But even with this we stand at the very beginning, a beginning which gives us a picture with which to characterize the attitude brought by external, abstract culture towards the first concrete statements that come from the spiritual world. When the representatives of current recognized knowledge hear what we have to say about the spiritual world, the understanding they bring to bear on what we say is of a kind that it can only be called a non-understanding. For it can be compared with the following: Suppose I were to write a sentence on this piece of paper, and suppose someone were to try to understand what I had written down by analysing the ink in which it is written. When our contemporaries write about Anthroposophy it is like somebody analysing the ink of a letter he has received. Again and again we have this impression. It is a picture very close to us, considering that we took our departure from a description of how, for human beings, in early post-Atlantean times even the starry constellations and starry movements were no more than a written expression for what they experienced as the spiritual population of the universe.

Such things are said today to a certain number of people in order to give them the feeling that Anthroposophy is not drawn from some sort of fantastic underworld but from real sources of knowledge, and that it is therefore capable of understanding the human beings of the earth to the very roots of their nature. Anthroposophy is capable of throwing light on today's differentiation of human beings into those of the West, of the middle realm and of the East, in the way mentioned yesterday. It is also capable of throwing light on differentiations which have existed in human evolution during the course of time. Only by connecting everything we can know about the differentiations according to regions of the earth with what we can know about how all this has come about can we gain an understanding of what kind of human beings inhabit our globe today.

Traditions of bygone ages have always been preserved, in some regions more, in others less. And according to these traditions the peoples of this globe are distinguished from one another. Looking eastwards we find that in later ages something was written down which during the first post-Atlantean period had existed unwritten, something which shines towards us out of the Vedas and their philosophy, something which touches us with its intimacy in the genuine philosophy of yoga. Letting all this work on us in our present-day consciousness, we begin to sense: If we immerse ourselves ever more deeply in these things, then we feel that even in the written works something lives of what existed in primeval times. But we have to add: Because the eastern world still lives within the living echoes of its primeval times it is unsuited to receiving new impulses.

The western world has fewer traditions. At most, certain traditions stemming from the third post-Atlantean period, the age of cosmosophy, are contained in the writings of some secret orders. But they are traditions which are no longer understood and are only brought before human beings in the form of incomprehensible symbols. But at the same time there is in the west an elemental strength capable of unfolding new impulses for development.

We might say that originally the primeval impulses existed. They developed by becoming ever weaker and weaker until, by about the fourth post-Atlantean period, they so to speak lost themselves in themselves, in what became Greek culture as such. Out of that, pointing towards the new, developed the abstract, prosaic sober culture of the Romans. (The lecturer draws on the blackboard). But this in turn must take spirituality into itself; it must, by becoming ever stronger and stronger, be filled with inner spirituality. Here, then, we have the symbol of the spiralling movement of humanity's impulses throughout the ages.

This symbol has always stood for important matters in the universe. If we have to speak of an atomistic world, we should not imagine it in the abstract way common today. We should imagine it in the image of this spiral, and this has often indeed been done. But on the greatest scale, too, we have to see this spiralling movement. Today I consider that we have arrived at it in a perfectly elementary manner by way of a concrete consideration of the course of human spiritual evolution.

LECTURE FOUR

Mannheim, 19 January 1922

Some time has passed since we met here, and the opportunity to discuss a number of things with you after such a long while gives me the profoundest pleasure. Behind us lie extremely grave times, difficult times, of which the gravity is certainly felt, though in wider circles it is still insufficiently understood. It is true to say that people who have experienced the second decade of the twentieth century have gone through more than is otherwise experienced over a span of centuries. We are asleep in our souls if we fail to notice how everything to do with human evolution is different now than it was ten years ago. The whole great turnabout that has taken place will no doubt only be fully realized by mankind at large after some time has passed. Then we shall come to see how the events that took place so catastrophically at the surface of life reach deep down into the roots of human souls, and how what has happened came about in the first instance as errors of soul affecting the widest circles of mankind. Not until the decision is made to seek in human souls the true reasons for this great human misfortune will it be possible to reach a real understanding of this time of trial undergone by mankind. Then also an attitude will develop towards a spiritual stream such as Anthroposophy which will differ from that prevailing at present.

This anthroposophical spiritual stream wants to give to mankind the very thing that has been lacking over the last three, four, five hundred years, the thing whose lack is so intimately bound up with the wretchedness of culture and civilization we have experienced and are experiencing. Both the greatest and the smallest matters and events in the world come out of the spiritual realm, out of life in the spirit. Universal questions face mankind today, questions which can only be tackled out of the depths of spiritual life, yet they are being dealt with in the most superficial manner all over the world. There is no possibility of seeing what it is that is struggling to rise up from the depths of human soul- and spiritual life. Yet it is just this possibility which Anthroposophy wants to bring to mankind.

Today I shall speak out of the realm of the anthroposophical world view about some intimate aspects of human soul- and spiritual life. Then, from the point of view this will give us, perhaps we shall be able to conclude with a brief consideration of some recent historical events.[1] Anthroposophical spiritual science wants to speak about those worlds which for the moment are hidden from external sense perceptions and also from the intellect which is attached to these sense perceptions. It wants to speak primarily about everything connected with the eternal aspect of the human soul. We say of the realms into which this anthroposophical world view wishes to penetrate that they can only be reached if human beings step over the threshold of consciousness. What is meant is that the step over the threshold must be taken consciously, if knowledge about these supersensible realms is to be gained. For human beings step unconsciously over the threshold every time they go to sleep. We say of the threshold we cross daily, in connection with going to sleep and waking up, that it is guarded by the Guardian of the Threshold. In doing so we speak of a spiritual force known by the spiritual researcher to be as real as are the human beings we meet. We speak of the Guardian of the Threshold because in the present phase of mankind's development human beings really do need to be protected in their consciousness from crossing unprepared into the spiritual realms.

It is quite remarkable that something which human beings have to value above all else, something to which they belong with the deepest roots of their existence and without which they would lack true human worth, namely the spiritual world, has to be hidden from them at the moment. This is profoundly linked to the whole purpose of human evolution. Human beings would not be able to achieve their true nature during the course of evolution if they did not themselves have to work for and win the strength with which to approach the spiritual world. If unearned grace alone were to allow them to step over the threshold, then perhaps they would be lofty spiritual beings, but they would not be human beings in the true sense of the word. They would not be beings who win their way towards their own value. For to be a true human being in the universe means to be the instigator of one's own worth. To step over the threshold unprepared would lead to a kind of burning up of the human being, a kind of extinguishing of the human being. However, what spiritual science has to say about man's relationship to the spiritual world can certainly be grasped by normal understanding. It is quite possible to understand what has to be said about this out of the foundations of spiritual science.

Observe how someone sinks into a kind of unconscious state on going to sleep. Out of this unconscious state individual waves rise up into the world of dreams as though from the depths of the ocean. Even for those who are free of any kind of superstition or nebulous mysticism, this dream world is mysterious, enigmatic, and it has to be sensed as belonging to the inmost being both of the world and of man's existence. So the period human beings spend between going to sleep and waking up is a kind of lowered consciousness out of which is revealed the picture world of dreams. And even if we only follow the dreams in an external manner, we still have to say: They contain picture echoes of that life which is not only given to us through our sense perceptions by way of our intellect, but also through our feelings. But they contain that otherwise familiar world in a way that is different. On the whole, they do not contain any abstract thoughts; they change everything into pictures. While the sense-perceptible world we know has a certain coherence and order which satisfies our understanding, so that everything has its place in space and time, dreams appear to shake everything up. Events which took place yesterday are mingled with others which happened decades ago. Dreams impose an order on things that differs from the order of space and time into which we look with our daytime consciousness.

Examining dreams more closely, we find that what is missing in them is our power of thinking. On waking up we feel that we step from dreamless sleep into the world in which human ideas and thoughts arise. We feel that we pour the picture world of dreams into our bodily nature. And as we do so our body sends out the power of thought which once more brings order into what the dreams have jumbled up. Our body takes us in hand when we wake up; our body gives us the power of ideas, and in dealing with this power we become fully awake. Then the world of dreams fades and its place is taken by the world of thoughts and ideas in the normal order of place and time.

Those who pay attention to these phenomena can observe in ordinary life how something, at first indeterminate, slips into our bodily nature. They can also understand this to the point where they can say: The power of thoughts is given to me by my body when I plunge down into it with my soul- and spirit-being. This everyday observation will bear out what Anthroposophy has to say: The ideas and thoughts we know in ordinary daily life are bound to our external physical body, which remains in bed at night when our being of spirit and soul steps over the threshold into another world. As consciousness is extinguished it leaves behind at the threshold the power and capacity to form a world of thoughts in the ordinary way. What steps over the threshold is whatever the human soul contains by way of feeling and will.

This content of feeling and will resembles the sleeping state even during ordinary day consciousness. We are properly awake only in our thoughts and ideas. Just think how dark is all that lives in our feelings, and how utterly obscure is everything living in our impulses of will. If we try to gain an idea of how we accomplish even the simplest decision of will, then what takes place in our muscles and bones when we put an idea into realization remains as obscure as our sleeping state. First we think: I lift my arm. Then we see our arm rising up. Nothing but impressions. The mysterious processes that take place remain as hidden from our consciousness as sleep itself. What we take with us across the threshold is, basically, something that is asleep and dreaming, even in our waking state. The dream pictures are no clearer than the feelings which attach to our world of thoughts and ideas. The forms in which soul life expresses itself—in the waking state through feelings and in the sleeping state through dreams—differ, but our life of feeling is no clearer than the pictures of our dreams. If it were clearer, we would lead an extraordinarily abstract life. Consider how we speak quite rightly of cold, sober thoughts and glowing feelings! But what lives in our feelings remains in a kind of darkness similar to that of our dream pictures.

When we go to sleep we carry our feelings over the threshold, and it is our feelings which, in a way, even light up to some extent in our dream pictures. We also carry our will into that world; it is as deeply asleep during our daytime as it is when we sleep. So we can say that what carries human beings through the threshold of consciousness is the feeling and will element of their soul being. Feeling and will belong to sleep consciousness. The life of thoughts and ideas and also a part of the life of feelings—because dreams light up—belong to the waking consciousness of daytime; they lie on this side of the threshold. We speak of the Guardian of the Threshold because it is necessary, at their present stage of consciousness, that human beings do not step consciously but unprepared over the threshold which they cross unconsciously every time they fall asleep. When we come to recognize the forces within which human beings find themselves on the other side of the threshold, we also learn to experience why they have to be guarded—prevented by a Guardian, by something which watches over them—from stepping unprepared over the threshold into the spiritual world.

When we enter the world beyond the threshold it certainly looks very different at first glance from what we have been in the habit of expecting. However, if we enter after having undergone sufficient preparation, it gradually changes and we come to new experiences, different from those we encountered initially, which are bewildering even for those who enter the spiritual world after some preparation. For what is it that appears to us first in the spiritual world? Forces, beings, are what first appear to us. And they behave—I cannot express it otherwise—in a very inimical manner towards the ordinary world of sense perceptions. As we step over the threshold into the spiritual world we are met with a burning, scalding fire which seeks to devour everything the world of sense perceptions has to offer. We enter, without a doubt, the world of destructive forces. This is the first sight that meets us on the other side. From the facts as they are I want to give you an idea of what it is like when we first step over.

Look at the human physical body which clothes us from birth to death. Now look, first with regard to the physical body, at the moment in which the human being approaches death and steps across the threshold. Looking simply at the world of space we find that, after the individual has crossed the threshold, the physical body appears externally much the same as it did before. But very soon we notice that this physical body, which has maintained its natural form for decades, is dissolved, destroyed by the forces of the external world, the external cosmos. It is the destiny of this body that it should be dissolved, destroyed by the forces of the cosmos. Simply by looking without prejudice at the fact, once the soul has departed, the body is destroyed and dissolved by the forces of nature, we must become convinced that between birth and death something not belonging to the world of sense perception lives in it which prevents its destruction. For if it belonged to this same world it would destroy the body instead of preserving it. If people would only take account of this obvious fact they would not find it so difficult to enter into anthroposophical spiritual science. There is the corpse; the external forces of nature destroy it. If what we bear within us were of a kind with the forces of nature it would destroy this body all the time. These simple thoughts are for ever disregarded.

Now bear in mind that we are permanently surrounded by a world which destroys our physical body. The moment our body is deserted by our soul it is destroyed. When we leave this body on going to sleep, we enter the world which destroys our corpse. This we have to come to recognize [*gaps in the shorthand report*]. We enter the world of destructive forces when we go to sleep, and yet this is the spiritual world. Why? Those who expect to find something beyond the threshold which resembles what is to be found here in the physical world of the senses are simply expecting to find another physical world beyond the threshold. But if spirit is to be found there, then the physical world of sense perceptions cannot also be there. What we experience there will have to be forces which have the inclination to destroy the physical world of the senses. This we experience in full force when we cross the threshold consciously. We experience with full force that in this spiritual world we find what is for ever inclined to destroy the physical world.

Now if we were to cross the threshold unprepared and unguarded, we should like it very much in that world—if I may put it simply. Especially would our lower instincts be most satisfied, and we would grow into this world we immediately meet, this world of destructive forces; we would become the allies of these destructive forces. We would no longer want to share in the work of maintaining the physical world which surrounds us. We have to learn to love this physical world as one which is filled with wisdom, in order to be well prepared to enter into the spiritual world. Before taking up our place, so to speak, at the side of the creators, we have to learn to love their creation and thoroughly understand that the world as it has been created has not been brought forth meaninglessly by divine, creative forces. In order to enter well prepared into the spiritual world we must first have thoroughly understood the meaning of earthly life. Otherwise on waking up every morning we would return to the world of sense perceptions filled with a terrible hate for this world and with an urge to destroy it. Simply out of the necessity of human existence we would wake up full of hate and anger if we spent the time between going to sleep and waking up in a state of consciousness such as that.

You can pursue this train of investigation further by looking at dreams in an unprejudiced way. Dreams are filled with terribly destructive forces. What comes to the surface in the form of dream pictures destroys every shred of logic. Dreams say: That's it, logic is finished, I don't want any logic! Logic is for the external world of sense perceptions; there it dogmatically arranges everything. Away with logic—a different world order is what is required! That is what dreams say. And if they were not only strong enough to caress our brain but were also able to submerge themselves into our whole body, then they would seize not only our logical instincts but also all our other instincts and our emotional life. Just as they destroy logic, so would they also destroy the whole life of physical human beings. We should be reluctant to enter once more into our physical body, and in doing so we would gradually destroy it. Because what lives in dreams is overcome by what meets it from the body, it comes about that logic is only destroyed momentarily. This can be observed in every detail. What continue during sleep are the forces which belong to our rhythmic system. Breathing continues, heartbeat and pulse continue. But thoughts cease, the will ceases. What belongs to our middle region continues, though in a subdued form. The moment the pulse grows a little weaker in the brain, dreams rush in and set about destroying the forces of the body—of logic—until these forces of the body once more overcome the dreams as the pulse gains in strength.

When it is a matter of really understanding these forces Anthroposophy knows very well how to be materialistic. Materialists do not really know how to be materialistic because they do not know how the spiritual realm works together with the physical. They fail to notice how the spirit enters into the physical and there continues to work. It is most interesting to observe how the spirit enters in and first wants to make itself felt and destroy logic. For then the forces of the physical body, its powers of thought and ideas, enter the fray and overcome it again. Dreams are rendered harmless to physical, earthly life. If you consider this properly you will gain deep insight into the relationship between waking and sleeping, for it shows that we have to remain aware of our spiritual origin, that we have to sink down again and again into sleep, but that on the other hand, in the present stage of our evolution, we have to be prevented from following in full consciousness what takes place in the state we enter between going to sleep and waking up.

We live on our earth. It is, in the first instance, a physical and a cosmic creation. A time will come when this earth will suffer death by fire. It will go through actual physical fire when the forces of destruction will seize hold of every earthly form, not only the corpses. Spiritual forces are leading this earth towards this death by fire, spiritual forces which are connected with the earth and which we meet in the first stage into which we enter when we step past the Guardian of the Threshold into the spiritual world.

Let us consider what we have gained with regard to stepping through the portal of death. Our physical body is entirely discarded. Our spirit and soul element now enters the spiritual world in such a way that it straight away develops the wish to return to the physical body. The element of spirit and soul, once it has laid down the physical body, can now begin to form a thought life without the physical body. While it lived in the body it was too weak to endure the forces of destruction. Now, as it passes through the portal of death, it has to be strong enough not to yearn for a return to the physical body. Since it no longer remains unconscious but, instead, enters a genuine consciousness as it passes through the portal of death it has to take up a certain kind of thought life, for only in the life of thoughts is it possible to become really conscious. This is the tremendous difference between crossing the threshold on going to sleep and passing through the portal of death. When we go to sleep our thought world is merely damped down until it returns when we re-enter our physical body on waking up. When we die we take up the thought life with our soul and spirit element without the mediation of our physical body. What does this mean?

Human beings would never return to their physical body in the morning if they knew the spiritual world, if they had grown to be part of it and did not have the wish, which is in them unconsciously, to return to their physical body, that is, to the physical world. Wishes, however, are something which is not connected with clear consciousness but which damp down this clear consciousness into a twilight. Human beings return to their body in the morning because of a wish, but it is these very wishes, pulling towards the physical body, which damp down their thought world. So they only find their thought life once again when they have returned to their body. But, in death, wishes have also died. Human beings enter the world-thoughts. As beings of spirit and soul they now have a thought life, but if they were to enter death entirely unprepared they would enter the same world as the one we enter when we go to sleep in the evening. To express this in extreme terms we have to say: If human beings enter death unprepared they find themselves in a terrible situation; for they have to watch what happens to their physical body. Their physical body is pulverized in the world-all, for if we do not cremate the body then it is cremated by the cosmos. And human beings would have to watch this happening if they were unprepared.

What is the consequence of this, and what has to happen so that human beings see not only destruction after death, so that they live not only in the midst of destructive forces? By absorbing spiritual content, by developing a world view which is consistent with the spirit, they must carry an inward relationship with the divine, spiritual world through the portal of death. If they are aware solely of a physical, material world, then they certainly enter after death in a state of terrible unpreparedness into the world of destructive forces as though into a world of scorching flames. But if they fill themselves with ideas and thoughts about the spiritual world, then the flames become the birthplace of the spirit after death so that they see not destruction alone; in the falling away of earthly dust from their human orbit they see the spirit rising up. No one should say what ordinary materialistic ideas are so prone to saying: I can wait until death comes to me! No, we must bear our consciousness of the spiritual world with us through the portal of death. Then with our soul and spirit we can overcome the destructive cosmic forces which take over our body, so that our element of spirit and soul rises up with new creativity above the destruction.

I am telling you this on the basis of anthroposophical spiritual science, but you have all, surely, heard of the fear experienced in former times in a sense of doom with regard to death, a sense of doom about which the Apostle Paul[2] taught when he spoke about man's soul being saved from falling a prey to death. In former times people knew that they could not only die physically with their corpse, but also spiritually with their soul. Human beings dislike speaking about the possible death of their soul. When speaking of death Paul does not mean physical death. He means something that can happen because physical death wants to lead on to the death of soul and spirit. Human beings must become aware once more that they have to do something during their physical earthly life in order to join their consciousness to their soul and spirit, so that these may carry something through death, in order that the spirit may arise for them out of the devouring flames which are always present after death.

Considerations like this must make it clear that to live within the whole universal order is an immensely serious matter. No view of the world is worthy of the human being if it does not lead through inner strength to a world of moral values, if it does not put before our souls the utter seriousness of life. To speak of physical and chemical forces building up the earth and of living creatures and, finally, man developing along the way, is not merely a one-sided world view; it is a world view which ignores the seriousness of life and which arises, actually, simply out of human laziness. A world view, on the other hand, which achieves a proper attitude to the spirit, leads to a seriousness about life because it puts before the soul the possibility that on passing through the gate of death the human being might become united with the forces of destruction. Throughout their physical life human beings are given the opportunity to prepare themselves suitably, because every evening as they go to sleep they are shielded from seeing the world of destructive forces to which they are related. They are given time to take in something that can guide them through the portal of death in a manner which enables them to discern the spirit within the forces of destruction. It is impossible to overemphasize the fact that feelings and perceptions about life must follow as a matter of course from a world view, and that a world view must not be allowed to remain mere abstract theory but must become something living, something which seizes hold of feelings and will. Civilized mankind must wrestle again for a world view such as this. Then, once more, what is imperishable will be seen within everything perishable; and, furthermore, out of everything that does not pursue its course egoistically within man it will be possible to push forward to eternity and immortality.

From this point of view look at life as it is carried on today. And do not take offence when someone who has to speak honestly is forced to say such disagreeable things. Look, for instance, at religious education. What is it built on? On egoism! Because people want to live beyond death, immortality—the possibility of going through death consciously—is spoken about. People long for this, and so to satisfy them—because it is disagreeable to appeal to knowledge—knowledge is omitted and mere belief is called into play. In this way, human egoism alone is approached, human egoism that wants to see what it will be like after death, instead of waiting till it happens. What it is like before birth is not found to be interesting. This can only be learnt through knowledge. Indeed, eternity—what comes after death and what stretches back beyond conception—can only be found through knowledge.

Even our language shows that we only have a half knowledge about the eternity of man. We speak only about immortality, 'undyingness'. What we need in addition is a word denoting 'unbornness'. Only when we can grasp both will we finally understand the eternity of the human being. Right down into language, human beings of our time have abjured their links with the spiritual world. These links must be found once more. If they cannot be found it will be totally impossible to carry on living in a proper way, and today's culture and civilization could fall into absolute decline.

In Stuttgart we have founded the Waldorf school[3] and Waldorf education. All sorts of things are said about this. Recently somebody said: Why does Waldorf education take so little account of fatigue in the children? Fatigue ought to be carefully studied nowadays. In so-called experimental psychology it is pointed out with pride how children tire after repeating unconnected words or following lessons about a sequence of subjects. And then it is said: Waldorf education is not up to date because it does not take the fatigue of the children into account. Why is this? The Waldorf school does not speak much about fatigue. But it does speak about how children ought to be tended and educated after the change of teeth, namely by basing the education mainly on the rhythmic system—which means that the artistic element is cultivated, since this is what stimulates the rhythmic system. Abstract writing comes later, and abstract reading later still. Demands are made, not of the head but of the artistic realm. But those who work with children only at those things which make demands on the head will, of course, have to reckon with fatigue. When, however, we make claims on the rhythmic system, on the artistic element, then we are justified in asking: Does our heart tire throughout life? It has to go on beating, and we have to go on breathing. So Waldorf education need not concern itself too much with fatigue because it aims to educate children in a way which tires them very little. Experimental education has arrived at a system which tires the children dreadfully; by its very method it brings about this tiredness. [*Gaps in the shorthand report*.] Waldorf education is concerned with body, soul and spirit, and account is taken of what comes from the spiritual and soul worlds to unite with the body and what departs again at death. Anthroposophy is the very thing which can help us to understand the material, physical realm.

What is most lively of all in the child? Its brain activity! From the brain the forces which mould the whole body stream out. These are most lively until the change of teeth. At the change of teeth this moulding capacity is transferred to the system of breathing and heart, and until puberty this is what we have to work with, which means that artistic work, not theoretical work, is what is required. Between the seventh and the fourteenth year the muscles are formed inwardly in a way which is adapted to the rhythmic system. Not until the fourteenth year approaches do soul and spirit take hold of the whole human being, and it is interesting to observe how until this moment the muscles have taken their cue from heartbeat, pulse and breathing. Now, through the sinews, they begin to make friends with the bones, with the skeleton, and to adapt themselves to external movements. You should learn to observe how young people change at this age. [*Gaps in the shorthand report*.] The process starts from the head; the soul element grows further and further towards the surface of the human being and takes hold of the bones last of all; it fills the whole human being and uses him up, making friends ever more closely with the forces of death, until these forces of death win through to victory at the moment of death.

Anthroposophical spiritual science follows up the spiritual processes right into the minutest detail, showing how they become immersed in material life and how they take hold of the whole human being, starting with the head. Not until knowledge such as this is taken into account, will it become possible to educate people properly once again. We need intellect and understanding so that we may find freedom, but they drive away the certainty of our instincts. A friend of mine was quite a nice person when we were young. Later in life he invited me to visit him. I had never partaken of a midday meal with scales and weights on the table. My friend first weighed everything he ate! By his intellect he had discovered how much he needed in order to maintain his body, and this exact amount was what he ate. Intellect drives out instincts in small things, but also on a larger scale. Now it is necessary for us to find our way back to them. A sure sense for life, a firm stand in life, is needed once more. This is found by seeking our eternal element within the temporal sphere; we need to understand how the eternal finds its place in the temporal. This is what our contemporary civilization needs.

Such things must be treated on a global scale. No account is taken these days of the contrasts that exist between people of the West and people of the East. External matters are broached in an external manner; congresses are called to discuss ways of balancing out the world's difficult situation, but no account is taken of the fact that East and West can only achieve economic balance if they have trust in one another. Asians will never be able to work together properly with the West if they cannot understand each other. But understanding can only come about through the soul. Understanding out of the soul is needed for the economic realm in the world; and understanding out of the soul can only be achieved through a deepening of soul life.

This is why today the most intimate matters of individual soul life are at the same time matters of worldwide import. Comprehension of what the world today needs, in external public matters too, will not be achieved unless an effort is made to listen to what the science of the supersensible has to say, for the world has changed during the course of evolution. The human race, in particular, has changed.

Looking at the span of human evolution, let us turn to that event without which the whole of human and earth evolution would have no meaning: the Mystery of Golgotha. In this Mystery of Golgotha something divine entered into the conditions of the earth by means of an earthly body. Christ entered the body of Jesus of Nazareth in order from then on to work with the earth. The earth would have perished, would have decayed in the world order, if a new fructification had not been brought about by the entering-in of the Christ. You know also that in the distant past an instinctive knowledge, a primeval wisdom, existed, of which only remnants remained in western civilization at the time of the Mystery of Golgotha. Enough remained, however, to make it possible for the Mystery of Golgotha to be at least instinctively comprehended for four centuries. In the early centuries of Christianity the understanding of the supersensible significance of the Mystery of Golgotha was such that the leading Christian teachers knew about the entering-in of Christ, the Sun Spirit, into the human being, Jesus of Nazareth.

Who today has a living awareness of what it means to ask whether the human being Jesus of Nazareth bore two natures, a human one and a divine one, or only one? Yet in the early Christian centuries this was a vital question, a question which had a bearing on life. There was a vivid awareness of how, coming from the cosmos, the Christ Spirit had united with Jesus; two natures in one personality; God in man.

You have often heard that the fourth post-Atlantean period lasted from 747 before the Mystery of Golgotha to about 1413 after the Mystery of Golgotha. In the first third of the fifteenth century intellectualism proper began. Now, we look at physical forces, we calculate, we study physics, but we no longer know that spiritual forces are at work out there, that the spirit which was known in earlier times really exists out there. Look at this fourth post-Atlantean, period lasting from 747 BC until 1413 AD. If you halve this period you come to a point that lies in the fourth century AD, the point when the wisdom which still contained a spiritual comprehension of the Mystery of Golgotha finally faded away. From then on, intellectual discussion was all that took place. And finally, as the fifteenth century approached, the human intellect became the sole ruler of human civilization. Because of this, anything that represented a living connection between the human being and the Christ was drawn more and more into merely materialistic human thinking. In the most advanced theology in the nineteenth century the Christ was entirely lost, and the most enlightened view was taken to be that of Christ as nothing more than the 'man of Nazareth'. If we can really feel this in all its gravity, we cannot but develop a yearning to find the Christ Being once again. And this yearning to find Christ once more is what the anthroposophical world view wants to satisfy with regard to the major global questions. In Central Europe people are particularly well prepared for this, as all kinds of symptoms show.

One of Western Europe's great thinkers, Herbert Spencer,[4] wrote about education in a way which pleases materialists very much. He said that all education is useless if it does not educate human beings to educate others. On what does he base this? He says: The greatest achievement in a human being's life is to beget other human beings. So therefore education must also be greatly important. From one point of view western thinking is correct. But what does an eastern thinker say? Out of the eastern spirit, something very ancient still lives in Vladimir Soloviev.[5] For western culture, primeval wisdom has disappeared. In the East it remains as a feeling. Soloviev still bears something of true Christian wisdom. Here in Central and Western Europe we have only a God-consciousness. There is virtually no knowledge of the Son. Harnack,[6] for instance, speaks of God in a way which makes it seem as though Christ, the Son, has no place in the Gospels. Consciousness of the Father, consciousness of God, is all that is left. What is said of the Son must also be said of the Father. But Soloviev still has something of the Christ-consciousness, and when he speaks it can sometimes be felt as if we were listening to the old Church Fathers from before the time of the Council of Nicaea.[7] Even the titles of his works are quite different. For instance there is a treatise on 'Freedom, Necessity, Grace and Sin'. You would be unlikely to find a treatise on grace or sin written by one of the western philosophers—Spencer, for instance, or Mill, or Bergson, or Wundt! No such thing exists in the West; it would be quite unthinkable and indeed is not to be found.

The eastern philosopher, though, still speaks like that, saying: A life given to man on earth, a life in which there was no striving for perfection in truth, would not be a genuinely human life. It would be valueless, as indeed would the striving for perfection in truth, if human beings had no part in immortality. Such a life would be a fraud on a global scale. Thus speaks Soloviev, the eastern philosopher. And he goes on: The spiritual task of man only starts when he reaches puberty. This is the very opposite of what Spencer says! Spencer makes the begetting of offspring the goal of development. For the eastern philosopher, development only begins at that point. It is the same with every matter, including questions of economic life. This is how the western economist speaks today, without having any sense for what eastern people feel about economic life. Today's major questions require consideration on a historical scale, and we ought to realize that the great misfortune of mankind in the second decade of the twentieth century, the great challenge and the great trial, is that involving considerations of this kind. An entirely different treatment of life must rise up out of the depths of the soul. The great questions of life, those that lie beyond birth and death, must come to play a part in ordinary human life. The questions of the present time must be illumined by the light of eternity, otherwise people will hasten from congress to congress and sink ever further and further into misfortune.

LECTURE FIVE

Breslau, 1 February 1922

It gives me profound pleasure to be among our Breslau friends. We have been through grave times which have made it all too obvious that mankind today is in need of something which can enable further development to take place. These catastrophic times are the consequence of a loss of upward momentum in human evolution. But in the soil of Anthroposophy we are tilling forces which can serve us in building up a spiritual life. Therefore I shall not speak too much today about contemporary events, but rather about the knowledge which human beings need, knowledge which they must absorb into their moral impulses. A great deal lives in our soul of which we are hardly aware. But because it is there, and because our soul element is linked to our existence on the earth, it is very important for our life.

What weighs on human beings today is the discordance between what the soul really needs and what present-day science can supply. Scientific knowledge is very demanding, and we ought to ask ourselves what it is that it demands of human beings. One thing it demands, for instance, is that we should accept its view of the beginning and end of the earth. Take the Kant-Laplace explanation of how the world began. A glowing ball of gas was formed by chemical and mechanical forces; it cooled, and when it was cool enough the same mechanical forces brought about the further solidification of everything that later became the kingdoms of plant, animal and man. And as for the future of earthly life and existence, we are told of an end to all life brought about by a gradual re-warming of the earth. Scientists say that physical laws will lead to the death of the earth through overheating. The end of the earth stretches before us like a gigantic churchyard. Between the two extremes, of the chemical and mechanical beginning of the world and its death by warmth at the end, lie all our human aspirations and ideals, all the moral purposes we have ever had or are going to have. The question is, why do such ideals and aspirations arise by chemical and physical means in the first place, if all they are destined for is to perish in the general death by overheating? Of course we can retort that these are theoretical considerations which have little influence on ordinary life. But even if we prefer to evade such questions, they still remain as disharmonies which work right into the depths of our unconscious soul life. They lead to the anxious question: What is the point of our moral impulses, what is the point of our religious ideals, if the whole of earth evolution is doomed to destruction?

The way this question is put shows what I am getting at. For all our moral impulses and all our religious ideals would be nothing but an immense fraud perpetrated on mankind, they would be a terrible illusion, if they were destined to be buried in the cemetery of the earth. Eloquent examples already exist of the terrible effect of such soul moods brought about by purely scientific knowledge, but we are often not properly conscious of them. So the anxious question lives on in human hearts. Asking it from the point of view of natural science we have to say: We human beings grew out of nature and our moral ideals rose up in us; but they will perish with the earth. These moral ideals will perish in natural science. Natural science does not allow us to concede that our ideals have an independent, actual, reality. And even though this is no more than a theory, it nevertheless weighs heavily on the human soul.

This fatalistic world view is based, in the final analysis, on faith in the imperishability of material forces. But anyone trying to topple this dogma is considered mad. If this dogma were true, there would be no escape for moral ideals; they would simply be a picture of something that human beings have thought up and figured out. There would be no escape for these ideals if spiritual research could not find the means to give back to people a supersensible content for their consciousness. This is relevant today. And in this relevant matter we are living at an important turning-point of evolution. Those of you who know me are aware that I do not like saying such a thing, because any moment in time can be called a turning-point. We have to consider in what respect a certain moment is a turning-point.

Let us consider where the knowledge given by natural science can lead us. Look first at the human being in his external manifestation living in the physical, sense-perceptible world. If we do this in an absolute sense, we see no more than a corpse. If we leave everything aside except the physical, sense-perceptible being and if we allow only chemical and physical laws to work on this being, then, by following only the external laws of nature, the human being begins to disintegrate, to dissolve. The forces we recognize with ordinary knowledge destroy the human being.

This alone is enough to refute the materialistic world view. If we say that the external forces destroy the human being, this must mean that from birth onwards people have been gathering forces which resist this destruction. As it dissolves, the corpse is absorbed into the world which we perceive with our senses. It is amalgamated into the sense-perceptible world by the death forces of chemical and physical laws. But what takes place at death inwardly at the level of the soul cannot be perceived by external sense-perception. These inward processes of soul can only be experienced by direct vision in the realm where higher knowledge has its source. This vision shows that outside the body the inward soul element is united with the spirit, with all the spiritual forces that stream through the world, giving it strength. The soul which unites with the spirit after death is then bound up in the spirit in the supersensible world.

This is a fact which takes its place beside the fact of the corpse. In life the physical body was filled by the soul; in death it unites with the forces of nature. Anthroposophy leads us to a fact of life which is diametrically opposed to the fact of death. The merely theoretical statement of the eternal life of man can never be satisfying. But Anthroposophy introduces the fact that the soul unites with the spirit. The knowledge of natural science, on the other hand, leads only to the fact of death.

The higher sources of knowledge given by spiritual science lead us to what is revealed to the spiritual seeker in Imagination, Inspiration and Intuition. These stages of knowledge are described in my book *Knowledge of the Higher Worlds*[1] and also in *Occult Science*. In the first instance you will find that here are descriptions of stages of knowledge. However, more is given to the spiritual seeker than mere stages of knowledge. Just as natural-scientific knowledge is not just knowledge but also possesses other sides and aspects, so it is with higher knowledge.

Today I shall consider with you something that goes beyond Imagination, Inspiration and Intuition as stages of knowledge, something that I discussed, for instance, in the Vienna lecture cycle of 1914[2] about life after death, but now from a somewhat different point of view. The part of the human being that lives here on earth is a corpse which is united with external physical nature. And just as he is united with the mineral forces below, so is he also united with the higher hierarchies above. Just as in the corpse he grows together with the mineral forces, so above he slowly grows together with, and enters into, the hierarchies. Sometimes people say that they might as well wait until they die to find out what happens then. And they might as well wait to grow together with the hierarchies. This is all very well, but it is not actually the point. It is very important for the human being to grow into the hierarchies in the right way, for we have to admit that to start with he stands in the world in a manner which allows him no inkling of his relationships with the higher hierarchies. Much depends on our becoming aware of these relationships.

The first hierarchy with whom human beings have a relationship we may call the world of the angels. But those who do not recognize the spiritual world—for whatever reason—cannot establish a relationship with the world of the angels, any more than someone who lacks physical sense organs can establish a relationship with the physical world. Angels are the beings next above man, closest to man, yet under certain circumstances we cannot approach them. Only by endeavouring to make a picture of the angel world while we are here on earth can we prepare to form relationships with it. The portal of death leads to the world of the angels if human beings can become conscious after death of what is confronting them.

The second group of higher beings is that of the folk spirits, or archangels. Angels are not folk spirits. Real folk spirits have no individual links with human beings, as is the case with angels. Folk spirits are related to communities and groups of human beings. Even natural science sometimes speaks of the national spirit, but this does not denote an actual being, let alone a spiritual one. From higher knowledge the spiritual seeker knows that folk spirits are real spiritual beings whose position is one step above that of the angels. The human being can grow into this hierarchy, too. But if our inner spiritual experience is not intense enough, our angel cannot lead us with our consciousness to the folk spirit. But since we have to be led to the folk spirit, this happens unconsciously by means of the laws of karma. Either we grow into the folk spirit consciously and with love, or we are forcibly led into the sphere of the folk spirits. When, after death, the moment is reached at which we turn to descend once more to the sense-perceptible world for a new incarnation, then it makes a great difference, as our soul is led down, whether we have consciously united in love with the folk spirit, or whether, unaware of what is going on, this takes place forcibly, under coercion.

This finds expression in a spiritual, a soul, fact. We can be born into a nation because we are related by coercion to that folk spirit, or because we are related by inner love. Those who are able to perceive such things find it outstandingly characteristic of our time that a great many people today lack a sufficiently loving relationship to their folk spirit. This statement hints at the cause for what today brings about disorder among nations. The conflict prevailing among nations today stems from the fact that many people are born with little love for their folk spirit and therefore find themselves in a forced relationship to it. The love which leads us to a particular folk spirit can never bring about a conflict with other nations. We must do everything we can to help people regain a love-filled relationship with their folk spirits. This is most urgent.

As we stand here in life, we have Imagination, Inspiration and Intuition as stages of knowledge which can lead to real vision in the spiritual and soul realm. But in the realm of spirit and soul, when our soul is to return once more to the physical world, Imagination, Inspiration and Intuition are facts governing events, they are facts of action. There our soul stands in a relationship with whatever it is that it has to achieve out of the cosmos. If we are to manage our life properly it must grant us conditions which make the achievement of its aims as nearly feasible as possible. Thus the discarnate, spiritual human being works through Imagination, Inspiration and Intuition towards his reincarnation in the physical world, while the incarnated, sense-bound human being can gain through Imagination, Inspiration and Intuition a vision of the world of soul and spirit.

Natural-scientific knowledge is not in a position to recognize the profoundest secrets of life. Such knowledge starts, for instance, with the consideration of a chemical compound. Proceeding to the consideration of a more complicated chemical compound, and so on, it arrives in the end at the living cell, which it regards as nothing more than a particularly elaborate chemical compound. Spiritual science shows that externally the cell is indeed a particularly elaborate chemical structure; but when the living cell, the germ of a new life, arises in the mother's womb in such an elaborate fashion, the chemical laws are reversed and become chaotic. In the germ of the embryo in the mother's womb, in the germ of life, the chemical laws are suspended, reversed, and in the realm of nature this means chaos. Because the germ is chaos, the cosmos can work into it.

Between death and a new birth the human being has an inkling of this. In the first step on the way to a new incarnation Imagination is realized and leads towards reincarnation. In the second stage

Inspiration is realized, and this is a far clearer consciousness than our brain consciousness, for Inspiration is a cosmic force. A part of this cosmic force is breathed in, as it were, and streams towards the bodily nature without coming fully to consciousness, rather as is the case with the will. We are unaware of how our will moves our hand, yet our hand moves in the manner required. The spiritual human being approaching incarnation through realized Inspiration stands in relation to this realized Inspiration as does the incarnated human being to the air. When we think about our physical body in the ordinary way, we imagine it to consist of muscles, nerves, vessels, bones. We imagine the same of a corpse. The airy part of our organism we assume to be outside it rather than within. Although we know that we cannot live without air, we still do not consider it as so intimately a part of ourselves as, say, our skeleton. Yet it is a part of our organism. The air as it is outside us, and at the next moment within, only to be outside again at the next, is a part of our organism. It lives rhythmically in us. In a far more extended rhythm we live with the element of soul and spirit. Just as we breathe air in and out, so we also breath the element of soul and spirit in and out, though for the most part this takes place unconsciously. Physically, too, part of what happens through breathing takes place unconsciously. When the human being consisting of soul and spirit breathes in realized Inspiration, he takes a picture into his soul. He takes it into the dampened down part of his consciousness. And what he takes in is the world of moral and religious impulses. He takes this in as his conscience.

The third stage in the descent to a new incarnation is when the human being makes the transition to what his parents give him. In doing this he is enacting a realized Intuition. So you see that what can be achieved, while incarnated, by way of three higher stages of knowledge, is something that is accomplished as a real occurrence in the realm of soul and spirit on the way to incarnation. Here on earth we ascend to the spiritual world through Imagination, Inspiration and Intuition. And on our return from the spiritual world to incarnation we descend from the spiritual world through Imagination, Inspiration and Intuition. This is the counter-image, in the spiritual world, of the three higher stages of knowledge.

What does this show us? It shows us that Anthroposophy is not merely knowledge but something which is alive. Through Anthroposophy we strive for higher knowledge in order to grasp the reality of the higher realms of life and in order to fill our souls with the content of what lives in the spiritual worlds. Those whose common sense has helped them to understand what the spiritual seeker has to say, experience something else as well. They can say to themselves that human beings in the state of incarnation between birth and death are constantly counteracting the death forces at work in their body. The forces of death are forever present in the human body, but so are those forces which counteract the forces of death. They are there. If we did not bear the forces of death within us we should never have developed our understanding for our physical environment.

One of the most important facts given to us by higher knowledge is that our forces of intellect are bound up with our forces of dying. Death is in a way nothing but a summary of all the forces of dying which are for ever at work in us. But a moral ideal, which can intensify until it becomes a religious ideal, lives in us in quite a different way. It is said that certain natural forces exist which bring it about that plants grow upwards; and these forces are taken to be quite real. But when, on looking into the human being, people find there the driving forces of moral and religious ideals, they are not inclined to accept these as having any reality. Yet there they are, working not only in every human being but also in the cultures of all mankind. Higher knowledge teaches us that moral ideals live in man through the burning up of matter. Matter is destroyed when a person makes moral resolves. The breaking down of matter is the precondition for the building up of moral ideals. What is crucial is the manner in which a human being breaks down matter and the manner in which he can build it up again. External research is still caught up in the prejudice about the indestructibility of matter. But spiritual science shows that man can break through external natural forces. Once we are in possession of an anthroposophical world view we can comfort ourselves in face of the idea of the death of the earth through overheating. For it is this very destruction of matter which ensures for the human being the possibility of building up his moral personality.

If you look deeply into your soul you will find something which consumes and gnaws at the soul of modern man. This something, which consumes and gnaws at the soul, is the fact that modern natural science excludes the moral element from the realm of what is real. Anthroposophy shows how human beings break through natural laws; how the moral element destroys matter, which is then built up again as matter which can be the bearer of a moral world order. All that is contained within the confines of our skin is connected with the dying forces of matter. But what the world builds up again—this has been forgotten by the natural sciences.

In order to discover new moral worlds we must proceed to the question of where matter can be built up. Death is in us at every moment, but so is resurrection. This is where we should look. This, out of the anthroposophical world view, is the perspective we must place before human souls, since the natural sciences have turned their attention for far too long and far too one-sidedly to the forces of dying. It is important to develop the courage to attend to what must be done in order to build up new worlds.

I am assuming that these suggestions will give encouragement and lead to meditations on how to see more clearly what is felt and talked about a great deal, but what ought also to be strongly willed.

LECTURE SIX

Dornach, 11 February 1922

Today[1] I should like to discuss a theme which can perhaps lead to some points of view from which to assess present-day cultural and spiritual life in connection with what has gone before in human evolution. As I have often said, cultural life since the first third of the fifteenth century is entirely different from that of earlier times, and now we are faced with the necessity to return, but in full consciousness and with deep thought, to an understanding of the spiritual part of our life in the cosmos. The spiritual part of our life in the cosmos was understood in ancient times by an instinctive clairvoyance, and this was the case most of all in the most ancient ages of earthly civilization. Then the capacity to push through to the spirit receded more and more, until a time came when mankind needed a new impetus, whereupon the Mystery of Golgotha took place.

Today I should like to mention that, before the Mystery of Golgotha, people who were concerned with spiritual life looked to those institutions known in general human cultural life as the Mysteries. In those most ancient days of human evolution it was unthinkable that spiritual vision and spiritual knowledge could have any other source than the Mysteries. When we try to observe the consciousness of those who turned to the Mysteries in those ancient days, if knowledge was what they desired, we arrive at the following picture: All external knowledge not stemming from the Mysteries, all intellectual knowledge gained by human beings by themselves, did not come into being until the later part of the Greek era. Only then did people want to discover certain truths out of themselves, without the help of the Mysteries. That is why the course of scientific development is reckoned, by those who understand these things, to have started in the time of Thales.[2] I have discussed this in my book *Riddles of Philosophy*.[3] Before that time knowledge was sought with the help of the Mysteries. When we examine the consciousness on which this was founded, we discover that those who conducted the Mysteries, and also their pupils, saw something most important in what they called 'the prince of this world'—they meant the earth—as opposed to the princes—that is, the spiritual beings—of other worlds.

In today's language, 'the prince of this world', as he lived in the consciousness of ancient times, would be called the being of Ahriman. The being of Ahriman would more or less be equivalent to this prince of earthly life. The spiritual revelations which can be derived from 'the prince of this world' are none other than those of intellectual knowledge. The leaders of the Mysteries would certainly have considered all that lived in the knowledge that grew up in Greece outside the Mysteries to have been inspired by 'the prince of this world'. In contrast, they saw it as the task of the Mysteries to lead human beings towards a spiritual vision which tends away from 'the prince of this world', which tends to lead human souls into realms which are not ruled by 'the prince of this world'. We cannot help but make use of such expressions in order to show properly what is meant, and no one should think that there is anything superstitious about using these expressions.

Let me give you a picture of what someone initiated in the ancient Greek, or the Egyptian, or Persian Mysteries would have thought in those old days about 'the prince of this world'. We have to understand that these people also spoke about the Christ-being, though they used other names. Using the name of Christ is not the only way of speaking about the Christ-being. We naturally use the name of Christ when we want to speak about the Christ-being, for Christ to us actually means that Being who underwent the Mystery of Golgotha and united himself with earthly civilization. Before the Mystery of Golgotha this Being was not yet united with earthly civilization. He still lived as the great Sun-being outside the earthly world. The Mystery of Golgotha denotes the uniting with the earthly world of this Being who lived outside the earthly world. But those initiated in the Mysteries certainly knew this Being who lived outside the earthly world. And the being known as 'the prince of this world'—that ahrimanic being—also knew him. That being—I am describing what lived in the consciousness of the initiates—felt himself to be the lord of the earth. He considered that whatever human beings possessed through the forces of the earth was something they had from him. But he knew that the Christ-being lived outside the earth and also had an influence on human life by way of the Mysteries, whose teachings were then popularized and brought amongst the peoples.

To describe more closely what lived in their consciousness, we may say that the initiates in the Mysteries thought as follows: The chief influence of 'the prince of this world' is on the physical bodies of human beings. These wholly do his bidding and he feels he is the lord of human physical bodies. But he could not feel himself to be the lord of the etheric and astral natures of human beings, of their life-bodies and their souls. The life-body and the soul were seen to be under the influence of a Being who lived outside the earth; the forces of the Christ-being had always been seen to flow into these. But with the forces of their own soul human beings were quite unable to receive what ought to flow into them from the Christ-being. They could only do so by turning to what the Mystery initiate received after the proper preparation. The Mysteries were seen to take hold of what came from outside the earth and pass it on to human beings. So 'the prince of this world' said to himself: Here on earth I am the master. From the earth the physical bodies of human beings draw their forces, and one of these forces is the human earthly intellect. Here I am the master and nothing can contest this here on earth. By way of the Mysteries, something from outside the earth flows into it. This I will tolerate.

But 'the prince of this world' rebelled against the Mystery of Golgotha because from then on he would have had to share his supremacy with the Christ who descended to the earth through the Mystery of Golgotha. 'The prince of this world' felt the Christ to be a rival in his mastery of the earth. He would have tolerated the sharing of the rulership with another being from outside the earth, but he would not tolerate a rival here within the earthly realm.

Here, then, out of the spirit of the ancient Mysteries, we have an indication of the real opposition of 'the prince of this world' towards the Christ. Among those with knowledge about such things this opposition was strongly felt throughout the Middle Ages until well into the fifteenth century. Any mention of 'the prince of this world' and of the Christ took it into account. There was a certain awareness of two dominions. One of these had rightfully ruled the bodily nature of man before the Mystery of Golgotha, but since then this sovereignty over the bodily nature of man has had to be shared with the other, with the Christ. For now Christ no longer influences only man's soul element, that is, his astral and etheric bodies; his purpose is now to influence also man's physical bodily nature, or rather whatever is expressed by this physical bodily nature, namely, everything to do with the intellect and with man's own capacities in the widest sense. Christ should live in every aspect of human nature. This is what entered into mankind through the Mystery of Golgotha.

Prior to the Mystery of Golgotha it never occurred to those who knew about such things to seek knowledge of external matters in any sphere which the human head or even the other soul or heart forces can reach on their own. Such things were left to the Mysteries. So before the Mystery of Golgotha there was certainly a strong awareness of the distinction between earthly wisdom and earthly sensing on the one hand, and a sensing of super-earthly forces on the other. The unique spiritual configuration of the early medieval centuries is only comprehensible in the light of a clear understanding of this fact.

Now this fact can be greatly clarified by something that was regarded as being of paramount importance in very many Mystery centres. The preparation and subsequent trials undergone by the Mystery pupils on the path of initiation varied, of course, in the different centres. But these variations were only really like the different paths up a mountain which, despite their different routes, all lead to one and the same summit in the end. They all led to one and the same Mystery goal. Despite the modifications, there were two measures within the Mysteries which every pupil had to undergo and which could be termed as being of paramount importance. These were, on the one hand, the draught of forgetfulness and, on the other hand, something which worked on the human being during the Mystery procedures like a powerful shock—like entering into a powerful fear. It is no longer permissible to use either of these for the purpose of achieving higher supersensible knowledge. Today everything has to take place in the realm of soul and spirit, whereas the Mystery pupils in ancient times underwent procedures which always had to call on their physical body. What is achieved today is similar, but higher knowledge must now be striven for in the sphere of consciousness only, whereas in earlier times it took place in the sphere of instincts and dreams. Because all the Mysteries included something akin to the draught of forgetfulness and also something akin to the physical shock, the pupils' external intellect was damped down. This intellect was less clear than it is today, but it nevertheless held sway in connection with everything relating to the external world.

So the pupil was led into a dulled consciousness both by the draught of forgetfulness and by the shock, which might be compared with the inducement of a state of fear. What was the significance of the draught of forgetfulness? The point was not the forgetting, though the pupil did forget. The effect it was to have came from its ceremonial preparation, from the special way it was mixed, to the accompaniment of certain preparations before it was drunk by the pupil. It was definitely a physical draught which, through the way it was served, brought it about that the pupil forgot the whole of his life since birth. This is something which is achieved nowadays through development in the realm of soul and spirit. Nowadays a clear consciousness of a great tableau of life encompassing everything that has occurred since birth is first conjured up. This is then suppressed and, in consequence, the human being is led into the spiritual form of his life before birth, or before conception. The same was achieved in a more physical way through the ancient draught of forgetfulness.

But the forgetting was not the essential point. Negative things are never the essential point. The positive thing achieved was that the pupil's thinking became more mobile and more intense. At the same time it became less clear. It became dreamy because the effect was achieved by influencing the physical organism. The effect of the draught of forgetfulness on the physical organism—it can be exactly described—was that the brain, if I may put it this way, became more fluid than it is in everyday life. Because the brain was made more fluid, because the pupil began to think more with his cerebral fluid than with the solid parts of the brain, his thoughts became more mobile and more intense.

Nowadays this must be achieved more directly, by means of developing soul and spirit as described in my book *Knowledge of the Higher Worlds* and in the second part of *Occult Science*. But in those days the brain was made more fluid by external influences. The goal was to make the spirit and soul element of the pupil—as it was before he made the connection with a physical body through conception: in other words, as it is in the spiritual world—capable once more of penetrating through the brain. This is the essential point.

In a drawing it would look like this. Suppose this is the mass of the brain (green). Once the human being has been born his spirit and soul element stops short before it (red). The brain is so constituted that the human being's inner spirit and soul element cannot pass through the brain. In his brain the human being is not filled with his spirit and soul element. Instead, external perceptions can enter and make themselves felt in the brain through the senses—let me draw an eye here. Put another way, the constitution of the brain is such today that the eternal aspect of the human being cannot rise up into it. Instead, external impressions can enter. By being given the draught of forgetfulness the pupil gained the possibility of receiving into his brain what was his spiritual and soul element before conception or

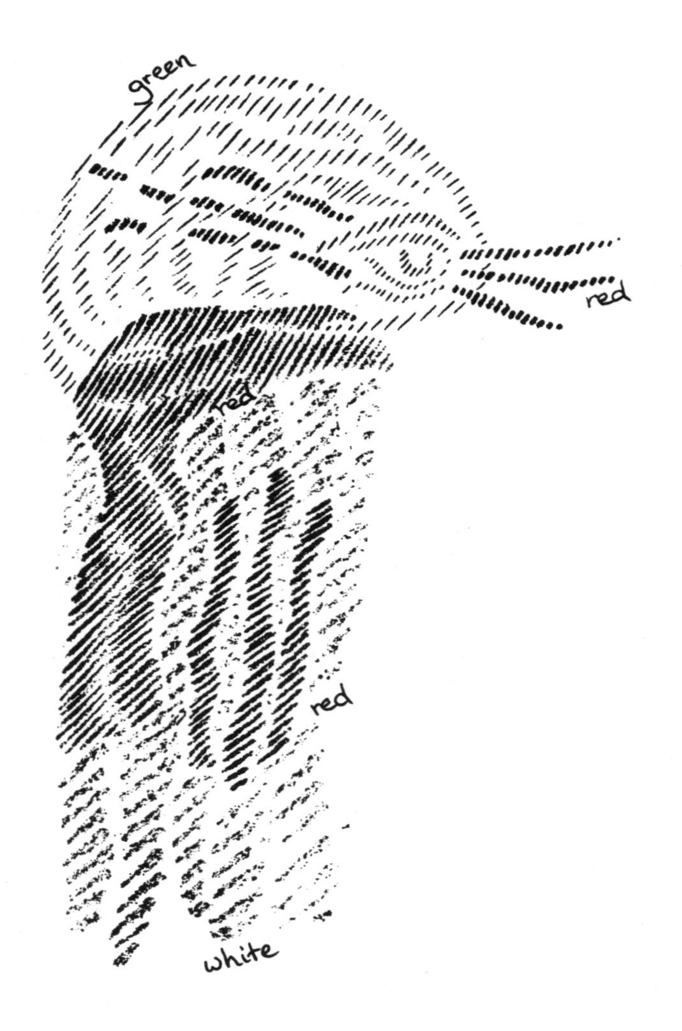

before birth (red). That is the one side.

The other side is the shock which was administered to the pupil. Think how a shock affects human beings. They are as though paralysed. There can be shocks which bring about the paralysis of the whole human being. A paralysed person, a cataleptic person, cannot move about because his muscles are rigid. But in a human being who can go about his life in the ordinary way, his body absorbs this eternal aspect (white with red). In our blood, in our muscles down below, the element of spirit and soul, the eternal element, is absorbed. But because of this it cannot be perceived. It cannot penetrate the brain, but lower down it is absorbed. It cannot be perceived, but when the muscles go rigid it steps out freely as a matter of course.

The rigidity of the muscles was brought about by the effect of the shock. As a result, the element of spirit and soul was not absorbed by the rest of the organism—apart from the brain—but was freed. So now the spirit and soul element was in the brain because the brain had been softened by the draught of forgetfulness, while the rest of the organism was at the same time prevented from absorbing it. Thus the element of spirit and soul came to be perceived. From two sides came the possibility of perceiving the element of spirit and soul. In ordinary life the human being was incapable of perceiving it because the brain, with which everything else was perceived, was unable to take it in; it could not enter the brain. Neither could it be perceived from the rest of the organism, the will and so on, for the rest of the organism had absorbed it. But now the pupil's brain was softened—of course, only for the moment at which knowledge was to enter. So his element of spirit and soul rushed into his brain. Meanwhile, the rest of his body became rigid so that it could not absorb the spirit and soul element. There the pupil stood, with his softened brain on the one side and a rigidified organic system on the other, as though encased in a capsule. There he stood in his spirit and his soul which had been given to him from two sides.

This is the aim of these procedures which are described in such a practical manner. I must expressly point out, though, that these things cannot be imitated nowadays. People would, anyway, be at a loss as to how to imitate them and, if they tried, the result would not be agreeable. These days all such things have to be attained by working with soul and spirit. But of the past it can certainly be said: Having been enabled to perceive their element of spirit and soul by partaking of the draught of forgetfulness and by being shocked into physical rigidity, the pupils in the Mysteries became 'Christians'. In the Mysteries they became Christians.

The early fathers of the church were certainly aware of this. But today people are not told about it, or it is even denied. But the early church fathers knew that human beings had been made Christians through the Mysteries. There are passages in the writings of the early church fathers[4] which state that Heraclitus and Socrates, though they lived before the time of the Mystery of Golgotha, were Christians, even though they were called atheists in their own time. I have often quoted from such passages in the writings of the early church fathers. It was the view of the ancient Mystery leaders and initiates that 'the prince of this world' was not interested in that human being who came forth out of the other; he left this human being to Christ. But he did not want Christ to come down to the earth in order to take hold of the human being in his entirety. This is described in the gospels in the way it is said that the demons, the lower servants of 'the prince of this world', when they heard that Christ had come, began to rebel. They recognized him and were furious.

We have to understand, when speaking about earthly evolution, that the spiritual powers whose influence on the human physical body was perfectly legitimate before the Mystery of Golgotha had, after the Mystery of Golgotha, to share this influence with the Christ. This is an essential aspect of the Mystery of Golgotha. That is why in the Middle Ages 'the prince of this world' came to be called 'the unlawful prince of this world'. This expression would not have been justified in the ancient heathen world but when it came to be used in the Middle Ages it was a correct title, befitting the circumstances.

The essential aspect of all this, with regard to the spiritual evolution of mankind, is that in more ancient times the physical body was withdrawn from the element of spirit and soul. The working of the brain was counteracted because the brain was softened by the draught of forgetfulness, and the powers of absorption of the rest of the organism were counteracted by the hardening of the rest of the organism by means of the shock. So in these older times the body was withdrawn from the element of spirit and soul.

Today, our aspiration is not to withdraw the body but to draw out the spirit, by strengthening and enhancing our forces of spirit and soul. The opposite of what used to take place must happen now; now the spirit must be drawn out. No changes must be allowed to take place in the physical, bodily aspect. Since the fifteenth century the human being has been organized in such a way that changes in the physical body, of the kind that were customary in those of Mystery pupils, would denote a condition of sickness. It would be a pathological condition, which must not be allowed to come about in normal development.

I am describing all this in order to give you an idea of what is to be understood by the concept of 'the prince of this world', which keeps recurring in olden times. 'The prince of this world', who in the Middle Ages became 'the unlawful prince of this world', is an Ahriman-like being. We can find such a being everywhere, in external nature and in the inner being of man. Indeed, only when we are in a position to find such a being in its manifestation both in external nature and in the inner being of man can we gradually come to an understanding of its essence.

Look at external nature. You will find there two contrasts, but what matters is to be able to sense the essence of these contrasts. Think of the blue sky. Of course in southern climes the blue sky must be seen rather differently than is the case here. When the envelope of air round the earth is filled by the effect of the sun, this is not the pure essence of the blue sky, for it is then overcast with something else. But the pure effect of the blue sky is that of coldness. The blue sky as such is cold. What you sense in the coldness of the blue sky, unmitigated by earthly sultriness—this is an all-embracing ahrimanic influence. The ahrimanic influence causes space to be petrified, congealed into blueness. Take note of this expression! It is unusual, but if you gradually come to sense what it means to say that space is petrified, congealed into blueness, you will have discovered the ahrimanic tendency in external nature.

The contrasting effect is that of the reddish, yellowish clouds sailing past. The effect is one of warmth, exactly the opposite. This, too, can be disguised by the coldness of the earth's environment but, all in all, a cloud lined with red, a yellowish cloud, has something warm about it. This is the contrasting effect, the effect of air. Between these two polar opposites something takes place, and that is what benefits the earthly life of man. We can say, then, that the effect on the earth of space petrified, congealed into blueness was seen in the Middle Ages to be the cosmic working of 'the prince of this world'.

And when we look into human beings we find that they can be in a condition which makes them pale. You know how there is something livid, something blueish about palor in human beings. When human beings turn pale, when they feel their way into coldness, they are then sensing something ahrimanic working in them. Flushed redness, on the other hand, shows something luciferic at work in their nature. Out of all these details together we can gradually build up a full picture of what this ahrimanic being, 'the prince of this world', really is. People's pallid, often so clever, thoughts, running along always in straight lines—the whole intellectual aspect of man—this is the ahrimanic influence, the influence of 'the prince of this world', on the working of the human head.

These things must be understood from the point of view of spirit and soul. In the livid blueness, in the way human beings grow pale, in the way they devour themselves inwardly and feel their way into coldness, in the way they are filled with pale, abstract thoughts—in all this we have to feel the ahrimanic influence, the rulership of 'the prince of this world'. And then we have to feel the warming influence of the Christ-impulse.

For the present time it is rather revealing and also necessary to recognize how different was initiation in ancient times compared with the principle of initiation today. There are certainly people today who still lack the courage to approach the Anthroposophical Movement but who have a deep longing for what, in the end, only the Anthroposophical Movement can give. They long for a transformation of their soul, after which they would find their way to the knowledge they seek. Obviously the greater part of mankind today rejects this transformation of the soul and imagines that any knowledge man is capable of reaching can be achieved through the ordinary state of soul which is brought about by our ordinary education and through our ordinary life. On my last tour I met a man who was greatly concerned to achieve some knowledge through the philosophical possibilities offered today, but not through Anthroposophy. He said that it would be interesting and important to ascertain in Anthroposophy how this higher knowledge might be achieved, for everywhere—this 'everywhere' is very relative, of course—the different world views were recognizing that the achievement of real knowledge was a matter not only of the intellect but also of the will. And in the ancient Mysteries, too, it was a matter of transforming the will.

In the description of the ancient Mysteries in my book *Christianity as Mystical Fact*[5] you will find that the decisive, radical difference between the ancient striving for knowledge and that of today lies in the fact that in ancient times it was necessary to prepare the will. The will had to be turned in a direction different from that of ordinary life. The will had to be purged, purified; it had to be transformed and lifted to a higher stage. The pupil had to give a new direction to his everyday will, which was dominated by 'the prince of this world'. Through cultivation of his will, the pupil had to reach the point at which knowledge can be attained. Today, on the other hand, people imagine that we can stop at whatever point we have reached through our ordinary studies. And our intellectual life is merely the product of the ordinary configuration of our brain. If it is softened, as I have indicated, there is a strong possibility that thoughts can be willed, that everywhere thoughts can be willed. And when will becomes conscious through the rigidifying of the body, then thoughts appear in the will itself. This can also happen today when, on the path I have described, knowledge of higher worlds has become possible.

It is a very important sign today that once more there are people who know that the intellect alone is not enough and that it is necessary to cultivate the will in order to reach whatever knowledge is possible for man. So by looking at what is going on in a general way we come to see that a great many people are approaching who want to hear about spiritual matters. Also, from things which are shown to us as we go along, we see that there are people who once again realize that the will must be cultivated, if knowledge is to be achieved. All this goes to show that there is an urgent need for spiritual life today. Unfortunately, though, because people lack the courage to approach Anthroposophy, because they think Anthroposophy is something peculiar, they imagine that they can achieve what they are searching for along some other path. The world will have to come to the conviction that what is wanted can only be achieved on the anthroposophical path. Please do not misunderstand me. It is not my intention to maintain that what Anthroposophy has revealed so far is necessarily generally valid or particularly obvious. But I want to point out the importance of the direction in which Anthroposophy is going. This is what can lead to the satisfaction of the powerful longing that exists today, a longing which must be satisfied if human civilization is to move forward at all.

LECTURE SEVEN

Dornach, 12 February 1922

Considerations such as those we embarked on yesterday are, of course, not necessarily set out for the purpose of inviting anyone to start practising what is needed for attaining supersensible knowledge. To a certain extent this intention is, of course, also present. But the main reason is to make known what kind of higher knowledge can be attained by such means. A declaration stating that one thing or another is possible in man's development is, at the same time, a declaration about the intrinsic nature of the human being. It can be stated that the human being seeking initiation is capable of extricating his soul and spirit element from his physical body, either by the means described yesterday with reference to the ancient Mysteries, or by means suitable for today, which I am about to discuss briefly. A statement such as this shows that the element of soul and spirit is an independent entity which has its own existence over and above that of the body. So a discussion about higher knowledge is, at the same time, a revelation about the being of man; this is, in the first instance, what is important for the dissemination of anthroposophical wisdom.

Yesterday I described how in the ancient Mysteries the bodily nature of man was treated so that it became able to free its soul nature in both directions. I said that the two main aspects of this in the ancient Mysteries were, on the one hand, the draught of forgetfulness, and, on the other hand, the occasioning of states of anxiety, fear, shock. The draught of forgetfulness, I said, wiped from memory everything pertaining to ordinary earthly life. But this negative effect was not the main point. The main point was that during the process of coming to Mystery knowledge the brain was actually made physically softer, as a result of which the spiritual element which is usually held off was no longer held off by the brain but allowed through, so that the pupil became aware of his soul and spirit element and knew that this had been in him even before birth, or rather, even before conception.

The other aspect was the shock which caused the organism to become rigid. When the organism grows rigid it no longer absorbs the soul and spirit element in the way it usually does with regard to its expression in the will. On the one hand the rigid bodily organism withdraws from the element of soul and spirit, and on the other hand the element of soul and spirit becomes perceptible to the pupil. Through the softening of the brain the thought aspect of the soul became perceptible to the pupil of the ancient Mysteries, and through the rigidifying of the rest of the organism the will aspect became perceptible. In this way, initiation gave the pupil a perception, a picture of the element of soul and spirit within him. But this picture was dreamlike in character. For what was it that was freed on the one hand towards the thought aspect, and on the other hand towards the will aspect? It was that part which descends from realms of spirit and soul to unite with the physical, bodily nature of man. Only by taking possession of the body can it become capable of making use of the senses and of the intellect. It needs the body for these things. Without the use of the body these things remain dreamlike, they remain dull, twilit. So by receiving his detached soul and spirit element as a result of the processes described, the pupil received something dreamlike, which, however, also contained a thought element.

As I said yesterday, if people were to follow these procedures today, the condition induced in consequence would be a pathological condition. For since the Mystery of Golgotha human beings have progressed in such a way that their intellect has become stronger by comparison with their earlier, more instinctive manner of knowing. This strengthening of intellectual life has come over mankind particularly since the fifteenth century. It is extremely significant that throughout the Middle Ages people still knew that in order to attain higher knowledge, or indeed to lead a higher kind of life, it was necessary to extricate the soul from the body.

If Schiller had managed to write a great drama he had planned, *Die Malteser* (The Knights of Malta), German literature would probably have been all the richer for a work on this medieval knowledge about the supersensible world, a work on the relationship of the Middle Ages to supersensible matters. It is a most interesting aspect of German culture that, precisely in the years when Napoleon destroyed the Order of the Knights of Malta,[1] Schiller was planning to write a drama about them, about the siege of Malta by the Turks and its defence by the grand master of the Order, de La Valette. Schiller was obviously prevented from writing this drama. He left it on one side and wrote *Wallenstein* instead. The Order of the Knights of Malta originated at the time of the Crusades. Schiller's drama would have shown clearly that the members of such an Order, which had the external task of working for the community and caring for the sick, considered that they could only do such work if they at the same time strove towards the attainment of a higher life.

At the time when the Order of the Knights Templar and the Order of the Knights Hospitaller of St John—which later became the Order of the Knights of Malta—were founded, and indeed throughout the Middle Ages, people had the certain feeling that human beings must first transform themselves before they can undertake such tasks in the right way. This is a feeling about the nature of the human being which has become entirely lost in more recent times. This can be put down to the fact that the human intellect has grown so much more intense and strong, with the result that modern man is totally intellectual because the intellectual aspect predominates entirely.

Now, in our own time, there is once more a great longing amongst mankind to overcome the intellectual aspect. Though literature and, above all, journalism, still express the opposite, nevertheless amongst the broad masses of mankind there is a longing to overcome the intellectual element. One thing that shows this especially is the fact that talks about spiritual matters are extremely well received in the widest circles. Another thing, even though it is not yet fully understood, is the way our eurythmy impresses the widest circles—not intellectually, but in what comes from the imaginative foundation of human beings. This became very obvious during my more recent lecture tours and especially the recent eurythmy tour. Eurythmy makes a very strong impression, even in circles where it cannot be understood in its deepest sense when it is seen for the first time. Nevertheless, it is felt to be something which has been called up out of the profoundest foundations of human nature, something that is more than what comes out of the intellect.

Now what is this intellectual element which is so much a part of the human being today? Let me draw you another diagram. As I said yesterday, with regard to the human brain (white), we can imagine how, as a result of the draught of forgetfulness, the element of spirit and soul, which usually came to a halt before penetrating too far inwards, now penetrated the brain (red). In the pupil of the ancient Mysteries the element of spirit and soul then rose up through the brain which had been thus prepared. Compared with ancient times, let us say prior to the Mystery of Golgotha, today's intellectual faculties are as they are because the element of soul and spirit is inwardly much stronger and more intense. The people of ancient times were far less intellectual. Their soul and spirit element was not etched with such sharp lines of thought as is the case today. Intellectuals think in straight lines, which is not how people thought in more ancient times. In those days thoughts were more like pictures, they were dreamlike and softer. Now, thoughts are endowed with sharp edges, clear contours. Yet, even though the element of soul and spirit is much stronger than it used to be, human beings today are still nevertheless incapable of grasping these thoughts with their soul and spirit element.

Please do not misunderstand me, my dear friends. Human beings today are considerably stronger in their soul and spirit than were people of old. They dream less than did people of old, and their thoughts are firmer. But their thoughts would be just as dull today as they used to be, if the element of soul and spirit alone were at work in them. Even today, human beings cannot think out of their soul.

It is their body which relieves them of the power of thought. Sense perceptions are received by the element of soul and spirit. But to think these sense perceptions we need the help of our body. Our body is the thinker. So nowadays the following takes place: The sense perception works on the human being; the element of soul and spirit (red, top) penetrates and mingles with the sense perception; but the body acts like a mirror and keeps on throwing back the rays of thought (arrows). By this means they become conscious. So it is the body which relieves human beings of the effort of thinking, but it does not relieve them of the effort of perceiving with their senses. So today, if human beings want to strive for initiation with regard to the thought aspect, they must turn their exercises towards strengthening their element of soul and spirit even more. We know these exercises from *Knowledge of the Higher Worlds* and from the second part of *Occult Science*. Thus will they gradually make their soul and spirit element so independent that it no longer needs the body.

So let us understand one another: When we think in ordinary life today, our element of soul and spirit does participate. Above all it takes in the sense perceptions. But it would be incapable by itself of developing the thoughts which are developed today. So the body comes along and relieves us of the effort of thinking. In ordinary life we think with our body, our body is our thinking apparatus. If we pursue the exercises described in the books mentioned, our soul will be strengthened to such an extent that it would no longer need the body for thinking but would itself be able to think. This is, basically, the first step on the path towards higher knowledge; it is the first step when the soul and spirit element begins to dismiss the body as the organ that does the thinking so far as higher knowledge is concerned. And it cannot be stressed often enough that a person who ascends to higher knowledge—that is, to Imagination—must remain at his own side with his ordinary good sense, keeping a watch on himself and being his own critic. In other words, he must remain the same person he always is in ordinary life. But out of the first person that second one develops, capable now of thinking without the help of the body, instead of with it.

The element of spirit and soul which revealed itself to the pupil

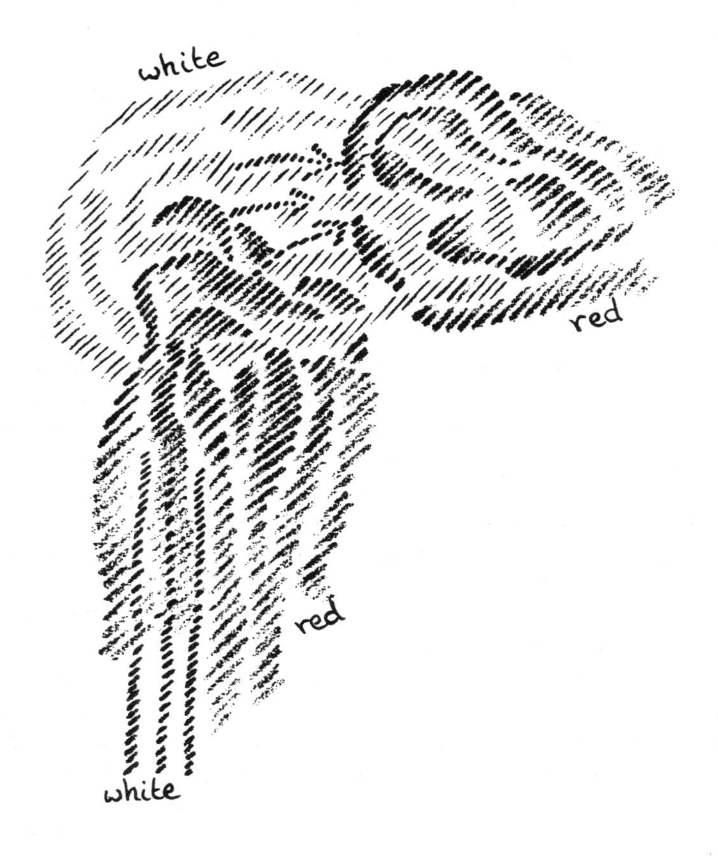

of the ancient Mysteries came out of the body and penetrated through the brain, and as it oozed forth the pupil perceived it. Today what is perceived in initiation is a strengthened thinking which does not in any way make use of the brain. The pupil in ancient times drew what he saw in the way of spirit and soul out of his own bodily organization. Today the human being perceives the soul and spirit element, as far as thoughts are concerned, in such a way that they penetrate into him in the same way as sense perceptions penetrate into him. In taking this first upward step towards higher knowledge the human being must accustom himself to saying: I am beginning to perceive myself with regard to my eternal element of soul and spirit, for this comes in through my eyes, it comes in from outside in every way.

In a public lecture[2] in the Bernouilli Hall in Basel I said: Anthroposophical spiritual science has to regard perception through the senses as its ideal. We have to take our start from perceiving with our senses. We must not return to dreamlike perception, but have to go forward to even clearer perception than that of perceiving with our senses. Our own being must come towards us, just as colours and sounds come towards our senses.

I showed two things in the last diagram. Both this (top) and this (bottom), the element of soul and spirit, are supposed to be one and the same thing. And they are one and the same, but seen from different sides. When a human being descends from the world of spirit and soul to physical incarnation, his element of soul and spirit, in a way, dies from the point of view of the soul and spirit world. When a human being is conceived and prepares to be born he dies as regards the spiritual world. And when he dies here in the physical world and goes through the portal of death he is born in the spiritual world. These concepts are relative. We die in respect of the spiritual world when we are born. And when we die in respect of the physical world we are born in the spirit. Death in the physical world signifies spiritual birth, birth in the physical world signifies spiritual death. Birth and death, then, are relative concepts. There is something which makes its appearance when the soul is on its way to birth, something that would not be capable of surviving in the spiritual world; it would disintegrate in the spiritual world, and so it streams towards a physical body in order to preserve itself.

In a diagram it can be depicted like this: The element of spirit and soul (red coming from the left) descends from the spirit and soul world. It arrives, you might say, in a cul-de-sac; it can go no further and is forced to equip itself with physical matter (blue). But the physical matter actually only works in the way I have described—from the brain, but not from the rest of the organism. As regards the rest of the organism the spirit and soul element does indeed travel onwards, having recovered through not being allowed to pass by the brain, through finding resistance and support in the brain. It is able, after all, to come to meet itself (red, right) throughout the rest of the organism, especially the system of limbs and metabolism. This blue part in the drawing is the head organism. Here (yellow) is the system

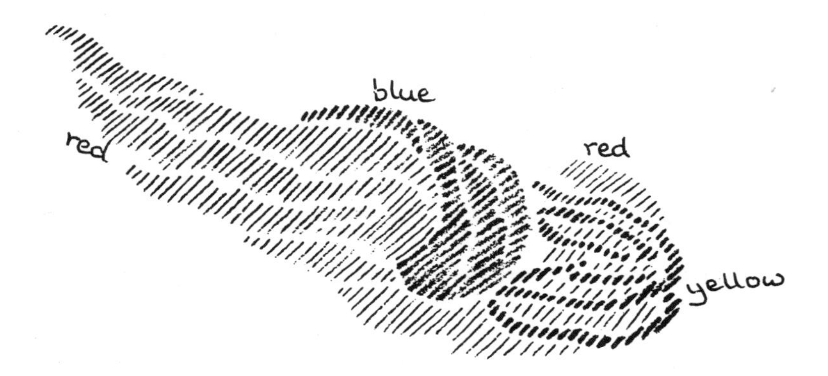

of limbs and metabolism; under normal conditions it absorbs the element of soul and spirit, but only to a certain extent.

As we grow up from childhood our spirit and soul element keeps making an appearance. At the moment of conception, and all through the embryonic stage in the mother's womb, the element of spirit and soul descending from the spiritual world is absorbed into matter. But because it finds a support it recovers again. Because of the shape of the embryo, at first that of the head, the element of spirit and soul finds a support (see drawing). Then the rest of the organism begins to grow, and once again the element of spirit and soul oozes through, as I have shown in the diagram.

As we grow up through childhood our element of spirit and soul gradually becomes ever more independent. I have often described this in detail and also shown how at major points of transition, such as the change of teeth and puberty, the element of spirit and soul becomes increasingly independent. As we grow up our physical body recedes more and more as we attain an independent spirit and soul element. This independent element is more intense today than it was in ancient times. But it would still be incapable of thinking. As I have said, it needs the help of the body if it wants to think. If this were not there, whatever grew towards us would remain forever dreamlike.

Initiates in ancient times strove to make their brain porous, so that what was then the element of spirit and soul could ooze through as it descended; in a certain way they could still see their life before birth through their softened brain. Today initiates are not concerned with that; they are concerned with what evolves during the course of life. This awakens a higher intensity with regard to the thought aspect. Initiates in ancient times would not have been capable of this. They would have been unable to take such a firm hold of the new spirit and soul element that begins to develop in the child—to begin with in an unclear way, and which later passes through the portal of death. In a way they slew the physical aspect, they paralysed it, so that the element of spirit and soul could emerge that had existed before conception.

Today we take a firmer hold of what we develop—at first in a weak way—through childhood and into adulthood, strengthening and reinforcing the new element of spirit and soul that has been developing since birth. We endeavour to achieve independence of our spirit and soul element over against our physical body, as far as our thought life is concerned. The pupil in ancient times made manifest the element of spirit and soul belonging to him before birth by toning down his physical body. We today endeavour to make manifest that element of spirit and soul which develops more and more from birth onwards. But we do not make it manifest to a degree which would be necessary in order to be able to see independently into the spiritual world. This is the difference.

As regards the will, the situation is as follows. The initiate in ancient times endeavoured to paralyse his will organization. This made it possible for him to perceive the element of spirit and soul he had from before his birth and which was normally absorbed by his will organization. If the body is rigid it does not absorb the element of spirit and soul, and so it is revealed independently. As modern initiates we do not do this; we do it differently. We strengthen our will by transforming the power of will in the manner described in the books already mentioned. It would be quite wrong to bring about a cataleptic condition by means of shocks or anxiety states as was the case in the ancient Mysteries. For modern man, with his highly-developed intellect, this would be something quite pathological. This must not be allowed to happen. Instead we use retrospective exercises—remembering backwards what has happened through the day—and also other will exercises to transform our will in a way which might be described as follows:

Consider the human eye. What must be its constitution if we are to be able to see? A cataract comes about when the physical matter of the eye makes itself independent so that it dresses itself up in physical matter which is not transparent. The eye must be selfless, it must be selflessly incorporated in our organism if we are to use it for seeing; it must be transparent. Our organism is most certainly not transparent for our will. As I have often said, we can think that we want to raise our hand. We form the thought: I want to raise my hand. But what then happens in our organism as this thought slips over into it and performs the action—this is as obscure for us as are the events which take place between going to sleep and waking up. The next thing we see is our raised hand, another perception. We perceive something at the beginning and we perceive something at the end, but what lies in between is a state of sleep. Our will unfolds in the unconscious just as much as the events of sleep unfold in the unconscious. So we can rightly say that for ordinary consciousness our organism is as untransparent as regards perceiving how the will functions as is an eye afflicted with cataract.

Of course I do not mean that the human organism is ill because of this. For ordinary, everyday life it *has* to be untransparent. This is its normal condition. But it cannot remain so for higher knowledge; it has to become transparent, it must become transparent for soul and spirit. This is achieved by means of the will exercises. Our organism then becomes transparent. We then no longer look down into something indeterminate when our will works, for our organism becomes as selfless as the eye, which is set selflessly into our organism so that we may perceive external objects properly. Just as the eye is in itself transparent, so our organism becomes transparent with regard to the element of spirit and soul; our whole organism becomes a sense organ. Thus, with regard to the will, we perceive the spiritual beings as objectively as we perceive external physical objects through our external eyes. Our will exercises are not aimed at making our body rigid in order to free our element of spirit and soul. They are aimed at developing the element of soul and spirit to such an extent that it becomes capable of seeing through the physical body. This is the main point. We see into the spiritual world only if we look through ourselves. We see external objects with our eyes only by looking through our eyes. And we do not see into the spiritual world directly, but only by looking through ourselves.

This is the other side: development with regard to the will. The whole of evolution in recent times depends, firstly, on our developing our thinking to an exent which makes it independent of the brain, and secondly, on our developing our will to an extent that the whole human being becomes transparent. It is impossible to see into the spiritual world through a vacuum, just as it is impossible to see the world of colours without looking through the eye. We have to look through ourselves, and this is brought about by means of the will exercises.

This, then, is for modern man what can be carried out by initiation. On the one hand, with regard to thinking, the element of soul and spirit can be made independent of the body, and on the other hand the material nature of the body can be overcome so that it becomes transparent for spirit and soul. Thus the element of spirit and soul has become independent through its own strength. This is the great difference between ancient and modern initiation. Ancient initiation transformed the physical body—the brain on the one hand, and the rest of the organism on the other—and, because the body was transformed in this way, the element of soul and spirit became faintly perceptible. Modern initiation transforms the element of spirit and soul, strengthening it with regard to the thought aspect on the one hand, and the will aspect on the other; thus it becomes independent of the brain, and at the same time so strong that it can see through the rest of the organism.

What the initiate saw in olden times appeared in ghostly form. Whatever beings of the spiritual world were able to reveal themselves when the procedure had been completed, appeared in a ghostly form. I could say that the spiritual world was seen in etheric shapes. The great anxiety of the teachers in the ancient Mysteries was that the pupils, despite the fact that what they saw of the spiritual world was ghostly, would learn to disregard this ghostly aspect. Ever and again they warned their pupils: What you are seeing appears to be material, but you must regard it as a picture; these ghostly things that you are seeing are only pictures of the spiritual world; you must not imagine that what you see around you in a ghostly form is actual reality. In a similar way, when I draw on the blackboard the chalk marks are not reality but only an image. Of course this expression was not used in olden times, but in modern terms it is a good way of putting it. It was the great concern of the teachers in the ancient Mysteries that their pupils should regard as pictures what they saw in a dreamlike, ghostly form.

In modern initiation there must be anxiety on a different score. Here, knowledge of the higher worlds can only be achieved at all by means of Imagination. Here we have to live in a world of pictures; the pictures have a picture character from the start. There is no danger of mistaking them in their picture character for anything else. But we have to learn to assess them correctly. In order to know how to relate these pictures to the spiritual reality they represent, we have to apply to them the exact thought processes we have acquired as modern human beings. We really have to think within this world of pictures in the very way we have learnt to think in the ordinary physical world. Every thoughtless glance is damaging to modern initiation. All the healthy ways of thinking we have developed as modern human beings must be brought to bear on higher knowledge. Just as we can find our way about the ordinary physical world if we can think properly, so can we only find our way about in the world of the spirit—which we enter through modern initiation—if we are able to penetrate with the thinking we have gained here in the physical world into all the knowledge we attain through Imagination, Inspiration, Intuition. In my book *Theosophy*,[3] as well as in *Occult Science* and *Knowledge of the Higher Worlds*, I have always stated categorically that this is a characteristic of modern initiation.

That is why it is so important that anyone who desires to enter into the higher worlds in a modern way should learn to think with exactitude and practise thinking with exactitude. This is not as easy as people suppose. To help you understand what I mean let me say the following: Think of something really startling: Suppose our present respected company were to be surprised tomorrow here in the Goetheanum by a visit from, say, Lloyd George[4]—of course this is only hypothetical, but I want to give an extreme example. If Lloyd George were to turn up here tomorrow you would all have certain thoughts and certain feelings. These thoughts and feelings would not be the result of simply observing all that went on from the moment of his appearance until the moment of his departure. In order to simply follow all this, you would not need to know that it was Lloyd George. If you did not know who it was, you would simply note whatever can be noted with regard to somebody who is entirely unknown to you. Until you learn to disregard everything you already know and feel from elsewhere about something you are observing, as long as you cannot simply follow what is going on without any of this, you are not thinking with exactitude. You would only be thinking with exactitude if you were capable—should Lloyd George really appear here tomorrow—of entertaining thoughts and feelings which applied solely to what actually went on from the moment you first noticed him to the moment when he disappeared from view. You would have to exclude every scrap of prior knowledge. You would have to exclude everything that had irritated you and everything that had pleased you about him and take in only whatever there was to take in at that moment. Only in this way is it possible to learn to think in accordance with reality.

Just think how far human beings are from being able to think with exactitude as regards reality! Only let something stir in your soul and you will see what feelings, living hidden and unconscious in your soul, you allow to rise up. It is extremely difficult to confine oneself solely to what one has seen. Read a description of something and then ask: Is the writer merely describing what he saw or is he not also calling up hundreds and hundreds of prejudices, both in feeling and in thinking, which are bound up with it? Only if you are capable of restricting yourself solely to what you have seen will you be in a position gradually to attain to thinking with exactitude.

It is necessary to lay aside everything we have been taught or have learned from life with regard to what we see, and follow solely what life presents to us. If you consider this and meditate on it a little you will gradually come to understand what I mean by thinking with exactitude. In ordinary life we have little opportunity under today's conditions to practise thinking with exactitude except in geometry or, over and above that, in mathematics. Here we really do restrict ourselves to what we see.

We have not many prejudices about a geometric form, a triangle for instance. Here is a triangle. Let me draw a parallel line here. This angle equals that angle, and the other one is equal to this one, and the one in the middle equals itself. This is a straight angle, so all three

angles of the triangle equal a straight angle. I am simply taking account of what I see before me, without applying the colossal prejudices I would bring to bear if Lloyd George were to arrive here tomorrow and I were to know about it in advance. In saying what I have just said, I was, of course, merely endeavouring to point out that thinking with absolute exactitude is a good preparation for seeing properly in the higher spiritual world. A kind of thinking in which you have firm control of the beginning of the thought, as well as a clear view of every step of thought along the way, is necessary in order to enter the higher worlds, that is, in order enter there with understanding. Above all a clearly-defined conscientiousness in thinking is necessary, a calling-oneself-to-account about one's thoughts. Ordinary life is very remiss in this, too. In most cases, people have no interest in thinking with exactitude; they prefer to think in a way in which they can enjoy the thought and feel comfortable with it.

For a Catholic priest, for instance, it is frightfully uncomfortable to entertain the thought that there might be something right about Anthroposophy. In such a case there can be no question of developing any exact thoughts. Instead, the matter is approached with all sorts of misconceptions and prejudices, and judgements are formed on the basis of these. Most things in life are decided on the basis of prejudices. Consider, for instance, what a strange impression is created sometimes when a simple attempt is made to describe something entirely objectively. Here we live in the Goetheanum. Nobody would consider me to be less of an admirer of Goethe than anyone else, and yet have I not said a good many things against Goethe? How often have I not attempted to describe Goethe from a narrow, overseeable point of view, whereas usually when Goethe is mentioned a whole host of prejudgements arises in response to his name alone. Merely to mention the name of Goethe sets up an excitement in the soul. It is impossible to approach any new phenomenon without prejudgement if one brings along a colossal collection of prejudices before even starting.

For the most part these things are not taken into account, and people therefore frequently say: Oh well, we can't get any further with our project of entering the spiritual worlds! Indeed, if elementary matters are not attended to first then, naturally enough, there is no way of entering those worlds. People just feel that unreasonable demands are being made of them if it is suggested that they take account of even the most elementary things.

Here is an example: In the nineties[5] I happened to be in Jena when Bismarck gave a grand speech after his forced resignation. He appeared on the platform in the wake of Haeckel and Bardeleben and other Jena professors. Imagine the huge crowd in the market square in Jena. They were expected to follow Bismarck's speech as they would a speech made by someone they had previously never heard of! Such a thing is unthinkable under normal conditions. And yet for someone who really desires to undergo a kind of initiation it is certainly necessary to develop an impartiality which enables him to take everything he sees as something entirely new, however many prejudices his soul might previously have harboured in that respect. Everything must be treated as though it had arrived like a bolt from the blue. For it is a special characteristic of the spiritual world that we have to win it afresh at every moment if we desire to enter it. And to do this we have to prepare ourselves in a suitable way.

It can be said that the general drift of civilization indicates that mankind is indeed headed in this direction. But for the moment this still appears in a light that is not all that pleasing, namely, in opposition to any kind of authority, and to any kind of received judgement, and so on. These things will have to be ennobled. But meanwhile mankind is indeed moving in the direction of impartiality and freedom from prejudice. But, for the moment, the more negative, the uglier sides of this are more prevalent. We must, therefore, judge the evolution of civilization with regard to the future in the very manner I have just been describing.

LECTURE EIGHT

Dornach, 17 February 1922

Today we shall consider the passage of the human spirit and soul through the sense-perceptible physical organism. We shall look first at how this element of spirit and soul prepares for physical incarnation by descending from the spiritual worlds, and then at how it departs from physical incarnation through the portal of death and returns to the spiritual world. We shall take particular account of what happens in the soul during this process, for we must understand that on entering the physical organism, right at the moment of conception, a tremendous transformation takes place, and that another tremendous transformation takes place when the human being departs from physical incarnation through the portal of death.

We have described these things from numerous standpoints already. But today we shall be concerned with the inner experience of the soul itself. What are the last experiences of the soul before it descends to physical life on earth?

Between birth and death our soul is filled with an intricate fabric of thoughts, feelings and impulses of will. All these work together and intermingle to form the total structure of the soul. Our language has words for all the different forms of thought, of feeling, and of will impulses, so that we can describe all these things that are experienced during physical earthly life. And by considering our more subconscious feelings and our soul experiences as a whole, we can throw at least some light on what lives in the soul before it enters earthly life.

First of all we must be clear that the thought element leads a shadowy existence in the soul during physical earthly life. Thoughts are quite rightly described as pale and abstract. At best, the thoughts and mental pictures of the human being during earthly life are no more than mirror images of the external world. Human beings make thoughts about what they have perceived with their senses in the external world. As you know, if you subtract from your thought life everything you have perceived through your senses and everything you have experienced with the help of your senses during the course of earthly life, there is very little left. This is different, of course, if a study of spiritual science has led to the acquisition of other kinds of thought content than those drawn from the sense-perceptible world. Our thought world is shadowy because it has lost its inner vitality as a result of our descent into the physical sense-perceptible world. You could say that as a solid earthly object is to its shadow on the wall, so is the real content of thoughts to what lives in our thinking during earthly existence. If we seek to make the transition from the earthly thoughts of our life between birth and death to the true stature of our thought life, we find that this really only exists in our purely spiritual life before conception has taken place. It is like going from a shadow picture to whatever is casting the shadow. Before birth, or rather before conception, there is a vivid, fully alive existence which later becomes shadowy thoughts. The thought world existing as an inner weaving of soul before conception might well be described as our actual spiritual existence, our actual spiritual being. This inner weaving life before conception is, of course, something that fills the whole of the universe known to us. Before conception we live throughout the totality of the universe which otherwise surrounds us. The thoughts that then live in us during our life on earth are the shadows, confined within our human physical organism, of something that has life on a cosmic scale prior to conception.

This is a description of one element of our soul before birth, or before conception. Before the human being descends to the physical world we find, as one part of the content of his soul, something that is like thoughts when he is on earth but which is actually a spiritual element of his being when he is in the supersensible world. The other part of the content of his soul cannot be described as anything other than fear, to use a concept taken from earthly life. In the period prior to physical life something lives in the soul which, as fear, fills it entirely. You must understand, however, that fear as an experience outside the physical body is something quite different from fear within the human physical body.

Before descending to earth man is a being of spirit and soul filled with an element of feeling which can only be compared with what is experienced in earthly life as fear. This fear is well justified for that period of human life about which I am now speaking. In the life between death and a new birth the human being has undergone manifold experiences of the kind which are possible while he is united with the cosmos. By the end of the life between death and a new birth he has, in a way, grown tired of this cosmic life, just as he grows tired of earthly life when, towards the end, his bodily organization shrivels up and becomes infirm. This tiring of life beyond the earth is expressed not so much in actual tiredness as in fear of the cosmos. The human being takes flight from the cosmos. He senses that the fundamental aspect of the cosmos is something that has now become foreign to him; it no longer has anything to offer him. He feels a kind of timidity, comparable with fear, towards the element in which he finds himself. He longs to withdraw from this cosmic feeling and contract into a human physical body.

From the earth a certain force of attraction comes to meet this state of fear in the human being. In a diagram it would look like this. Think of the cranium, and the brain within. Here is the base of the cranium. As I have frequently suggested, the human brain with its remarkable convolutions is a kind of copy of the starry heavens, of the universe. This brain structure made up of cells is indeed a copy of the starry heavens (see diagram). While living before birth in the cosmos the

human being encompasses with his spirituality the whole of the starry world. But now he fears it. He withdraws into an earthly image of the starry heavens, an image in the human brain.

Now we come to the choice made by man's spirit and soul. For now the soul chooses whichever brain—in the process of being formed—most closely resembles the starry constellation in which it stood before descending into the earthly realm. Naturally, the brain of one embryo depicts the starry heavens differently from that of another embryo. And the soul feels attracted towards the brain which has the most similarity with the starry constellation in which it existed before descending to earth.

So it is, in the main, a feeling of timidity which leads the soul down to the confines of a human being—a feeling of fearfulness with regard to infinity, you might say. This feeling of fear pertains more to the soul. And the thought world which unfolds more and more from childhood into adulthood pertains more to the spirit. Both—the feeling of fear and also the spiritual element which is transformed into shadowy thoughts—undergo a substantial metamorphosis which I should now like to describe to you. I can only use expressions which will seem unusual as far as ordinary thinking goes, but ordinary thinking lacks points of reference which might serve to describe these things. Ordinary thinking lies far from all aspects of this theme, so we cannot avoid using unusual expressions if we want to give an adequate description of them.

Let us start with the spiritual element which lives in the cosmos and then makes its way to the confined dwelling place of the human body, unfolding chiefly through the nervous system and the brain and undergoing metamorphosis as it does so. There are two aspects of this. First of all it is definitely true to say that the being who is man in the world of spirit and soul prior to conception dies during the transition into the physical body. Birth in the physical body is a dying for the spirit and soul life of man. And when a death takes place there is always a corpse. Just as a corpse remains when man dies on earth, so a corpse also remains when the element of spirit and soul goes down to the earth through conception and dies in the heavenly region. For the whole of our earthly life we then live, as far as our thoughts are concerned, on what remains as a corpse. The corpse is our world of thoughts. Something that is dead is the world of shadowy thoughts. So we can say that as the spiritual aspect of man descends to life on earth through conception, it dies for the world of spirit and soul and leaves this corpse behind.

Just as the corpse of the physical human being dissolves into the elements of earth, so the element of spirit and soul dissolves in the spiritual world and becomes the force which is unfolded in physical thoughts. Just as the earth goes to work on the corpse when we bury it, or as fire does when we cremate it, so throughout life we go to work on the corpse of our spirit and soul element in our world of physical thoughts. The world of physical thoughts is the continuing in death of what exists as real spiritual life before man descends into physical earthly life.

The other living element which enters into man from his pre-earthly life comes into play in the physical human being, not through the world of thoughts, but in the widest possible sense in everything which we can call feelings—feelings to do with man as well as feelings to do with nature. Everything by which you spread into your environment in a feeling way (see chart) is an element which represents a living echo of pre-earthly life.

You do not experience your pre-earthly life in a living way in your thoughts but only in your feelings for other creatures. If we love a flower or a person, this is a force which has been given to us out of our pre-earthly life, but in a living way. So if we love a person we can say that we love him or her not only out of our experiences in this earthly life, but also out of karma, out of being connected in earlier earthly lives. Something living is carried over from pre-earthly life in so far as the sympathetic sphere of the human being is concerned. On the other hand, what is a living spiritual element between death and a new birth dies into our thought world during earthly life.

Spirit — Dead thoughts
Spirit — Feelings of sympathy

Fear — Feeling of self
Fear — Will

That is why our thought world is so pale and shadowy and dead during earthly life, because it actually represents a part of our pre-earthly experience which has died.

Now let us turn to the second element—timidity, fear—which is also metamorphosed in such a way that it falls into two parts. What we experience prior to our descent into the earthly world as a fear which fills our whole soul and makes us want to flee from the spiritual world, becomes, on entering the body, on the one hand something that I should like to describe as a feeling of self. This feeling of self is metamorphosed fear. Transformed fear from pre-earthly life is what makes you feel that you are a self, that you are self-contained.

The other part into which fear is transmuted is our will. All our will impulses, everything on which our activity in the world is based—all this exists as fear before we descend into earthly life.

You see once again what a good thing it is for earthly life that human beings do not step consciously past the Guardian of the Threshold. I have frequently said that human beings sleep through what the will represents, down there in the human organism. They have an intention, then they carry it out, and then they perceive the consequence. But what lies between the intention to do a deed and the accomplished deed, that in which the will actually consists—this is something in which human beings are as much asleep as they are between falling asleep and waking up again. If they were to look down and see what lay at the foundation of their will they would feel, strongly welling up out of their organism, the fear coming in from their pre-earthly life.

This is also something that has to be overcome in initiation. But if we look into ourselves, the first thing we see is the feeling of self. This is something which must not be caused to increase too much as a result of the training. Otherwise, when the human being finally steps into the spiritual world he might fall into megalomania. But at the foundation of all his will impulses he will find fear and he must therefore be strengthened to withstand this fear.

As you see, in all the exercises contained in my book *Knowledge of the Higher Worlds* the aim is to learn to bear the fear which we come to perceive in the way I have described. This fear is something that has to be there amongst the forces of development, otherwise human beings would never descend from the spiritual world into earthly existence. They would not flee from the spiritual world. They would not develop the urge to enter into the limitations of the physical body. The fact that they do develop this urge stems from this fear of the spiritual world, which quite naturally becomes a part of their soul configuration once they have lived for a time between death and a new birth.

So thoughts are attached to us like a corpse—or rather the power of the thoughts, not the thoughts themselves. We can describe this even more exactly. However, to consider this more exact description it will be necessary to develop certain very precise ideas. The spiritual force which dies in our thoughts and becomes a corpse when we descend into physical earthly existence is the same force which builds our organs out of the cosmos. Our lung, heart, stomach—all our specific organs—are formed out of the power of thought of the universe.

When we enter into earthly life this power of thought enters the narrow confines of our organism. What does the earth and its environment want of us? It wants us to create an image of it within ourselves. But if we were to create an image in ourselves, then during the course of our lifetime all our inner organs, such as our lungs—but, above all, the manifold convolutions of our brain—would be transformed into crystal-like formations. We should all become statues resembling not human beings but crystals in various contrasting groups. We should gradually come to be inorganic, lifeless shapes—statues after a fashion.

The human organism resists this. It stands by the shape of its inner organs. It will not have it that, for instance, its lungs might be formed to represent, let us say, a range of mountains. It will not allow its heart to be transformed into a cluster of crystals. It resists this. And this resistance brings it about that instead of forming images of our earthly environment in our organs we do so only in the shadow images of our thoughts. So our power of thought is actually always on the way to making us into an image of our physical earth, of the physical form of our earth. We constantly want to become a system of crystals. But our organism will not permit this. It has so much which has to be developed in the living realm, in the realm of sympathy, in the realm of feeling of self and in the realm of will impulses, that it does not permit it. It will not allow our lungs to be transformed into something that looks like crystals growing out of the earth. It resists this formation into earthly shapes, and so the images of earthly shapes only come about in geometry and in whatever other thoughts we form about our earthly environment. As I said, you must think with absolute exactitude if you want to reach the point where you can imagine all this.

But the tendency is always there of coming to resemble the system of our thoughts. We have to fight constantly in order not to take on this resemblance. We are constantly striving to become a kind of work of art—though given the kind of thoughts human beings have on the whole, it would not be a very beautiful work of art to look at. But we strive to attain an external appearance that resembles what exists in our thoughts as no more than images and shadows. We do not achieve this resemblance, but we mirror back what we are aiming for, so that it turns into our thoughts instead. It is a process that can truly be likened to the creation of mirror images.

If you have a mirror with an object in front of it, then you get a mirror image of the object. The object is not inside the mirror. Everything we see before our eyes constantly wants to bring about an actual structure within us. But we resist this. We keep our brain as it is. Because of this, the object is mirrored back and becomes the mental image. A table wants to make your very brain into a table but you do not allow this to happen. In consequence an image of the table arises in you. This act of rejection is the mirroring process. That is why, in our thought life, our thoughts are only shadow images of the external world. When it comes to our feelings, however, the situation is different. Try once to imagine absolutely accurately what is involved in feeling something. A round table feels different from one with corners. You feel the corners. The thought of this angular table does not affect you very much, whereas getting the feel of the corners is more painful than gently following the curve of a round table. When we feel, therefore, external forms come more to life within us than when we think.

This is an indication of the metamorphosis undergone by our element of soul and spirit when it comes into earthly existence from pre-earthly existence. But now what occurs when we go through the portal of death? Our world of thought is, so far as its strength is concerned, only the corpse of pre-earthly existence. It is of little significance. It disappears when we go through the portal of death, just as our mirror image disappears if we suddenly take away the mirror. So, in speaking of immortality, there is absolutely no point in reflecting on the earthly power of thought for it certainly does not accompany us through the portal of death. What does go through the portal of death with us is everything we have developed in the way of sympathy, of feeling and sensing towards earthly things. Our feeling of sympathy goes through the portal of death. Inasmuch as we have sympathy towards our environment, we develop the strength (see table) in the spiritual world to stand among the spiritual beings in the spiritual element of

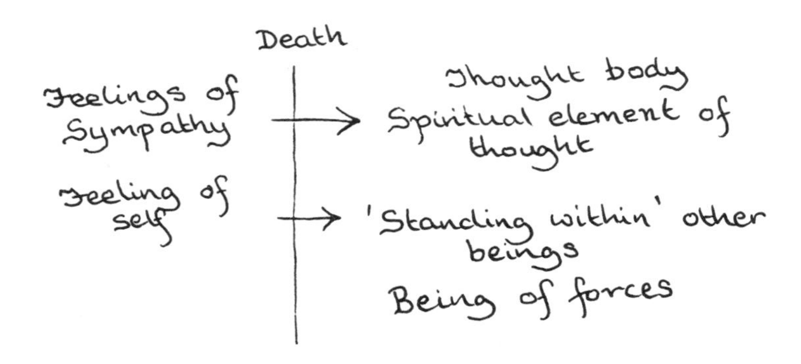

thought. Our sympathy, which our body keeps separate from our earthly environment, streams out now, after death, into our spiritual environment and unites with the spiritual thought element of the world into which we step on going through the portal of death.

Because we flow with our sympathy into the spiritual element of thought, we develop once again a kind of thought body, a living thought body which is ours for the time between death and our next birth. And the feeling of self we have on earth becomes a kind of 'standing within' other beings. Whilst we are on earth, our feeling of self only lets us know that we are within our body, but once we have passed through the portal of death we learn to know that we are in other beings, the beings of the higher hierarchies. And because we stand within spiritual beings we receive from them forces which lead us onwards on our course through life between death and a new birth. In this way our own being of forces develops. This is the metamorphosis of the element of spirit and soul which takes place when we pass through the portal of death.

Unlike our world of thought, our will does not disappear at death. It is the source of the content of our feelings of self. Imagine that you want something which satisfies you. This wanting in itself gives you something that satisfies you, it gives your feeling of self a particular nuance. If you have done something that does not satisfy you, this too gives your feeling of self a particular nuance. Our will is not only something that acts outwards. It also rays forcefully back into our inner being. We know what we are from what we can do. And this nuance of our feeling of self, this raying back into us of our will element, is something which we take into the spiritual world with us, together with our feeling of self. So we take our will—or rather the raying back of our will into our feeling of self—with us when we submerge ourselves in the beings of the higher hierarchies. And because we take with us this element, which has either strengthened or weakened our feeling of self, we find the force of our karma, our destiny.

Gaining an understanding of these things helps us to see what the human being really is. And we also learn to recognize certain symptoms which accompany earthly life. In earthly life fear certainly puts in an appearance here and there. But it must never be allowed to fill our soul entirely. It would be sad if this were to happen. But before we come down to earthly life our soul is indeed entirely filled with fear, and in that situation fear is what we need so that we really do descend into physical earthly life.

Our feeling of self, though, is something that must not be allowed to exceed more than a certain degree; indeed it really ought not to be felt independently at all in earthly life. Someone who develops his feeling of self with too much independence turns into a person who knows only himself. Our feeling of self is actually only with us during earthly life, so that we keep a hold on our body until we die, returning to it every morning after sleep. If we lacked this feeling of self during earthly life we would fail to return. But after death we need it when we become submerged in the world of spiritual beings, because without it we would all the time lose ourselves.

We do indeed submerge ourselves there in real spiritual beings. The earth, on the other hand, makes no such demands on us. If you go for a walk in the woods, you stay on the path, and the trees are to the left and right of you, and in front and behind. You see the trees but the trees do not expect you to enter into them—they do not expect you to become tree nymphs and submerge yourselves in them. But the spiritual beings of the higher hierarchies, whose world we enter after death—they do expect us to submerge ourselves in them. We have to become all of them. So if, on passing through the portal of death, we were to enter this spiritual world without our feeling of self, we would lose ourselves. We need our feeling of self there simply in order to maintain ourselves. And moral deeds we have done during earthly life, deeds which have justifiably enhanced our feeling of self—these protect us from losing ourselves after death.

These are thoughts and ideas which, from now on, ought to enter once again into human consciousness for the near future of earthly evolution. These thoughts and ideas simply flowed into mankind in earliest times, when understanding was still instinctively clairvoyant. Human beings used to have a strong feeling of what they had been before they descended into earthly life. This was strongly developed in primeval times. But hope of a life after death was less strongly developed in primeval times. This was something that was taken for granted. Today we are chiefly interested in what we might experience after we die. In primeval times, thousands of years ago, people were more concerned about their life prior to descending to the earth.

A time then came when clairvoyance, which had originally been instinctive, waned, and the intense connection of the soul with life before birth also waned. Then two spiritual streams sprang up which prepared what had now to develop in human civilization. We now have two clearly distinct streams which we have described from varying standpoints. Today we shall approach them from a particular standpoint which will also be a help to us in our considerations tomorrow and the next day.

Take earthly evolution prior to the Mystery of Golgotha. You find, spread over the earth, the heathen culture, and in a certain way separated from this, a culture which one could say was that of the Old Testament. What was particularly characteristic of this heathen culture? It contained a definite awareness of the fact that everything physical surrounding man contained a spiritual element. The heathen culture had a strong awareness of the nature of living thoughts which become transformed into dead thoughts. In the beings of the different kingdoms of nature, this culture saw everywhere the living element of which human thoughts were the dead counterpart. Heathen culture perceived the living thoughts of the cosmos and regarded man as belonging to these living thoughts of the cosmos.

One part of this heathen world that was particularly filled with life was that of the peoples of ancient Greece. You know that the idea of destiny was particularly strong in the world of these ancient Greek peoples. And—think of certain Greek dramas—this idea of destiny permeated human life with laws in the way the natural laws permeate nature. The ancient Greeks felt that they stood in life permeated with destiny, just as natural things stand permeated with the laws of nature. Destiny descended on human beings within this Greek outlook like a force of nature. This feeling was characteristic of all heathen cultures, but it was particularly marked among the Greeks. The heathen world saw spirit in all of nature. There was no specific knowledge of nature in the sense of the natural science we have today, but there was an all-embracing knowledge of nature. Where people saw nature, they spoke of the spirit. This was a science of nature which was, at the same time, a science of the spirit. The heathen peoples were less interested in the inner being of man. They looked on man from the outside as a being of nature. They could do this because they saw all the other natural things as being filled with a soul element too. They did not think of trees, plants, or clouds as soulless objects. So they could look at human beings from outside in a similar way and yet not think of them as being soulless. Filling all nature with soul in this way, the ancient heathen was able to regard human beings as natural creatures. Thus the ancient heathen world was something which contained from the start a spiritual element which inclined towards the world of spirit.

The creed which then ran its course in the Old Testament was the polar opposite of this. The Old Testament knew nature neither in the way we know it—I mean in the way we come to know it as we turn towards spiritual science—nor in the way the ancient heathen knew it. The Old Testament knew only a moral world order, and Jahve is the ruler of this moral world order; only what Jahve wills takes place. So in the world of the Old Testament the view arose as a matter of course that one must not make images of the soul and spirit element. The heathen world could never have come to such a view, for it saw images of the spirit in every tree and every plant. In the world of the Old Testament no images were seen, for everywhere the invisible, imageless spirit ruled.

We ought to see in the New Testament a coming together of these two spiritual streams. People have always given prominence to either one view or the other. Thus, for instance, the heathen element was always predominant where religion was more a matter of seeing the objects of religion. Pictures were made of spiritual beings, pictures copied from nature. In contrast, the Old Testament element developed wherever the newer scientific attitude arose with its tendency towards a lack of images. In many ways modern materialistic science contains an echo of the Old Testament, of the imageless Old Testament. Materialistic science strives for a clear distinction between the material element in which no trace of spirit is left, and the spiritual element which is supposed to live in the moral sphere only, and of which no image may be made, or which we may not be allowed to see in the earthly realm.

This particular characteristic which is prevalent in today's materialistic form of science is, actually, an Old Testament impulse which has come over to our time. Science has not yet become Christian. The science of materialism is fundamentally an Old Testament science. One of the main tasks as civilization progresses will be to overcome both streams and resolve them in a higher synthesis. We must understand that both the heathen stream and the Jewish stream are one-sided and that, in the way they still exercise an influence today, they need to be overcome.

Science will have to raise itself up to the spirit. Art, which contains much that is heathen, has made various attempts to become Christian but most of these attempts have fallen into luciferic and heathen ways. Art will have to lead to a Christian element. What we have today is but an echo of the heathen and the Old Testament elements. Our consciousness is not yet fully Christian. This is what we must particularly feel when we consider factually, as described by spiritual science, the way in which human beings pass through birth and death.

LECTURE NINE

Dornach, 18 February 1922

Let us recall the main points we considered yesterday. Through conception and birth into the physical, sense-perceptible world, the human being brings down on the one hand something which inwardly still possesses the living spiritual world, but which then becomes shaded and toned down to the thought world he bears within him. On the other hand he brings down something which fills his element of soul and spirit, something which I have described as being essentially a state of fear. I then went on to point out that the living spirit is metamorphosed into a thought element, but that it also sends into earth existence a living remnant of pre-earthly life that lives in human sympathy. So in human sympathy we have something that maintains in our soul the living quality of pre-earthly existence. The feeling of fear that fills our soul before we descend to the physical world is metamorphosed here on earth on the one hand into the feeling of self and on the other into the will.

What lives in the human soul by way of thoughts is dead as far as spirit and soul are concerned, compared with the living world of the spirit. In our thoughts, or at least in the force which fills our thoughts, we experience, in a sense, the corpse of our spirit and soul existence between death and a new birth. But our present experience during physical earthly life, of a soul that has—in a way—been slain, was not always as strong as it is today. The further we go back in human evolution the greater is the role played here in earthly life by what I yesterday described as sympathy—sympathy not only with human beings but also for instance with the whole of nature. The abstract knowledge we strive for today—quite rightly, to a certain extent—has not always been present in human evolution. This abstract inner consciousness came into being in its most extreme form in the fifteenth century, that is, at the beginning of the fifth post-Atlantean period. What human beings now experience in their thoughts was, in earlier times, filled with living feelings. In older knowledge—for instance, that of the Greek world—abstract concepts as we know them today simply did not exist. Concepts then were filled with living feelings. Human beings felt the world as well as thinking it. Only at the beginning of the fifth post-Atlantean period did people begin to merely think the world, reserving their feelings of sympathy for what is really only the social realm.

In ancient India human beings felt strong sympathy for the whole of nature, for all the creatures of nature. Such strong sympathy in earthly life means that there is a strong experience of all that takes place around the human being between death and a new birth. In thinking, this life has died. But our sympathy with the world around us certainly contains echoes of our perceptions between death and a new birth. This sympathy was very important in the human life of earlier times. It meant that every cloud, every tree, every plant, was seen to be filled with spirit. But if we live only in thoughts, then the spirit departs from nature, because thoughts are the corpse of our spirit and soul element. Nature is seen as nothing more than a dead structure, because it can only be mirrored in dead thoughts. That is why, as times moved nearer to our own, all elemental beings disappeared from what human beings saw in nature.

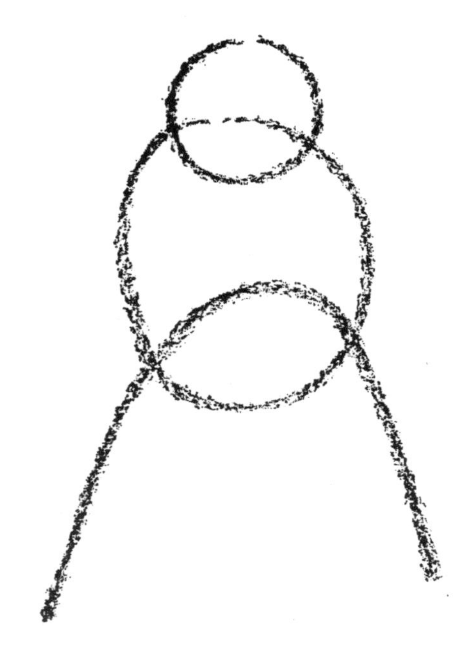

So what is this kind of spirituality that human beings still feel within themselves—this living spirituality—when, in reality, they ought to experience nothing but dead spirituality? To answer this question we shall have to consider what I have said with regard to the physical organization of the human being as a threefold organism. Here (see diagram) is the organism of nerves and senses, located mainly in the head. The rhythmical organism is located mainly in the upper chest organs. But of course both systems appear in the total organism too. And here is the organism of the limbs and the metabolism, which is located mainly in the limbs and the lower parts of the trunk.

Let us look first at the head organization which is chiefly, though not exclusively, the bearer of our life of nerves and senses. We can only understand it if we look at it pictorially. We have to imagine that our head is for the most part a metamorphosis—not in its physical substance, but in its form—of the rest of the body, of the organism of limbs and metabolism we had in our previous incarnation on the earth.

The organism of limbs and metabolism of our previous earthly life—not its physical substance, of course, but its shape—becomes our head organization in this life. Here in our head we have a house which has been formed out of a transformation of the organism of limbs and metabolism from our former incarnation, and in this head live mainly the abstract thoughts (see next diagram, red) which are the corpse of our pre-earthly life of soul and spirit.

In our head we bear the living memory of our former earthly life. And this is what makes us feel ourselves to be an ego, a living ego, for this living ego does not exist within us. Within us are only dead thoughts. But these dead thoughts live in a house which can only be understood pictorially; it is an image arising out of the metamorphosis of our organism of limbs and metabolism from our former earthly life.

The more living element that comes over from the life of spirit and soul, when we descend into a new earthly life, takes up its dwelling from the start not in our head, but in our rhythmical organism. Everything that surrounded us between death and this new birth and now plays into life—all this dwells in our rhythmical organism. In our head all we have is an image out of our former earthly life, filled with dead thoughts. In our rhythmical, breast organism lives something much more alive. Here there is an echo of everything our soul experienced while it was moving about freely in the world of spirit and soul between death and this new birth. In our breathing and in our blood circulation something vibrates—forces that belong to the

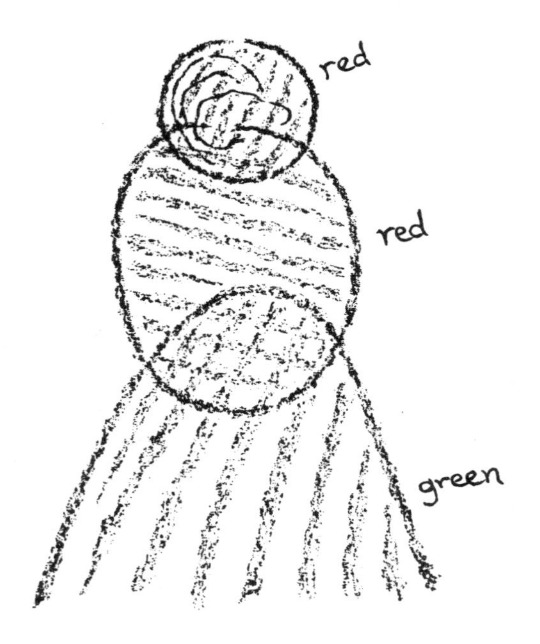

time between death and birth. And lastly, our being of spirit and soul belonging to our present earthly incarnation lives—strange though this may seem—not in our head, and not in our breast, but in our organism of limbs and metabolism. Our present earthly ego lives in our organism of limbs and metabolism (green).

Imagine the dead thoughts to be still alive. These dead thoughts live—speaking pictorially—in the convolutions of the brain. And the brain in turn lives in a metamorphosis of our organism from our former incarnation. The initiate perceives the way the dead thoughts dwell in his head, he perceives them as a memory of the reality of his former incarnation. This memory of your former incarnation is just as though you were to find yourself in a darkened room with all your clothes hanging on a rail. Feeling your way along, you come, say, to your velvet jacket, and this reminds you of the occasion when you bought it. This is just what it is like when you bump into dead thoughts at every turn. To feel your way about in whatever is in your head organization is to remember your former life on earth.

What you experience in your breast organism is the memory of your life between death and a new birth. And what you experience in your limbs and metabolism—this belongs to your present life on earth. You only experience your ego in your thoughts because your organism of limbs and metabolism works up into your thoughts. But it is a deceptive experience. For your ego is not, in fact, contained in your thoughts. It is as little in your thoughts as you are actually behind the mirror when you see yourself reflected in it. Your ego is not in your thought life at all. Because your thought life shapes itself in accordance with your head, the memory of your former earthly life is in your thought life. In your head you have the human being your were in your former life. In your breast you have the human being who lived between death and this new birth. And in your organism of limbs and metabolism, especially in the tips of your fingers and toes, you have the human being now living on the earth. Only because you also experience your fingers and toes in your brain do your thoughts give you an awareness of this ego in your earthly life. This is how grotesque these things are, in reality, in comparison with what people today usually imagine.

Thinking with the head about what happens in the present time is something that only became prevalent at the beginning of the fifth post-Atlantean period, in the fifteenth century. But in an ahrimanic way things are forestalled. Things that take place later than they should in the course of evolution are luciferic. Things that come too soon are ahrimanic. Let us look at something which came about in history very much too soon and should not have happened until the fifteenth century. It did happen in the fifteenth century, but it was foreshadowed at the time of the Mystery of Golgotha. I want to show you how the ideas of the Old Testament, which I partly described yesterday, were transformed into nothing more than allegories by a contemporary of Christ Jesus, Philo of Alexandria.[1]

Philo of Alexandria interprets the whole of the Old Testament as an allegory. This means that he wants to make the whole Old Testament, which is told in the form of direct experiences, into a series of thought images. This is very clever, especially as it is the first time in human evolution that such a thing has been done. Today it is not all that clever when the theosophists, for instance, interpret *Hamlet* by saying that one of the characters is Manas, another Buddhi, and so on, distorting everything to fit an allegory. This sort of thing is, of course, nonsense. But Philo of Alexandria transformed the whole of the Old Testament into thought images, allegories. These allegories are nothing other than an inner revelation of dead soul life, soul life that has died and now lies as a corpse in the power of thinking. The real spiritual vision, which led to the Old Testament, looked back into life before birth, or before conception, and out of what was seen there the Old Testament was created.

But when it was no longer possible to look back—and Philo of Alexandria was incapable of looking back—it all turned into dead thought images. So in the history of human evolution two important events stand side by side: The period of the Old Testament culminated in Philo of Alexandria at the time of the Mystery of Golgotha. He makes allegories of straw out of the Old Testament. And at the same time the Mystery of Golgotha reveals that it is not the experience of dead things that can lead the human being to supersensible knowledge, but the whole human being who passes through the Mystery of Golgotha bearing the divine being within him.

These are the two great polar opposites: the world of abstraction foreshadowed in an ahrimanic way by Philo, and the world which is to enter into human evolution with Christianity. The abstract thinker—and Philo of Alexandria is perhaps the abstract thinker of the greatest genius, since he foreshadowed in an ahrimanic way the abstractness of later ages—the abstract thinker wants to fathom the mysteries of the world by means of some abstract thought or other which is supposed to provide the answer to the riddle of the universe. The Mystery of Golgotha is the all-embracing living protest against this. Thoughts can never solve the riddle of the universe because the solution of this riddle is something living. The human being in all his wholeness is the solution to the riddle of the universe. Sun, stars, clouds, rivers, mountains, and all the creatures of the different kingdoms of nature, are external manifestations which pose an immense question. There stands the human being and, in the wholeness of his being, he is the answer.

This is another point of view from which to contemplate the Mystery of Golgotha. Instead of confronting the riddle of the universe with thoughts in all their deadness, confront the whole of what man can experience with the whole of what man is.

Only slowly and gradually has mankind been able to find the way towards understanding this. Even today it has not yet been found. Anthroposophy wants to open the gate. But because abstraction has become so firmly established, even the awareness that the way must be sought has disappeared. Until abstraction took hold, human beings did wrestle with the quest for the way, and this is seen most clearly at the turn of the fourth to the fifth post-Atlantean period. As Christianity spreads externally, the best spirits wrestle to understand it inwardly.

Both streams had come down from the far past. On the one side there was the heathen stream which was fundamentally a nature wisdom. All natural creatures were seen to be inhabited by elemental spirits, demonic spirits, those very demonic spirits who, in the Gospels, are said to have rebelled when Christ came amongst mankind, because they knew that their rule was at an end. Human beings failed to recognize Christ, but the demons recognized him. They knew that he would now take possession of human hearts and human souls and that they would have to withdraw. But for a long time they continued to play a role in the minds and hearts of human beings as well as in their search for knowledge. Heathen consciousness, which sought the demonic, elemental spirits in all creatures in the old way, continued to play a role for a long time. It wrestled with that other form of knowledge which now sought in all earthly things the substance of Christ that had united with the earth through the Mystery of Golgotha.

This heathen stream—a nature wisdom, a nature Sophia—saw the spirit everywhere in nature and could therefore also look at man as a natural creature who was filled with spirit, just as all nature was filled with spirit. In its purest, most beautiful form we find it in ancient Greece, especially in Greek art, which shows us how the spirit weaves through human life in the form of destiny, just as the natural laws weave through nature. We may sometimes recoil from what we find in Greek tragedies. But on the other hand we can have the feeling that the Greeks sensed not only the abstract laws of nature, as we do today, but also the working of divine, spiritual beings in all plants, all stones, all animals, and therefore also in man. The rigid necessity of natural laws was shaped into destiny in the way we find it depicted, for instance, in the drama of Oedipus. Here is an intimate relationship between the spiritual existence of nature and the spiritual existence of man. That is why freedom and also human conscience as yet play no part in these dramas. Inner necessity, destiny, rules within man, just as the laws of nature rule the natural world.

This is the one stream as it appears in more recent times. The other is the Jewish stream of the Old Testament. This stream possesses no nature wisdom. As regards nature, it merely looks at what is physically visible through the senses. It turns its attention upwards to the primal source of moral values which lies in the world between death and a new birth, taking no account of the side of man which belongs to nature. For the Old Testament there is no nature, but only obedience to divine commandments. In the Old Testament view, not natural law, but Jahve's will governs events. What resounds from the Old Testament is imageless. In a way it is abstract. But setting aside Philo of Alexandria, who makes everything allegorical, we discern behind this abstract aspect, Jahve, the ruler who fills this abstraction with a supersensibly focused, idealized, generalized human nature. Like a human ruler, Jahve himself is in all the commandments which he sends down to earth. This Old Testament stream directs its vision exclusively to the world of moral values; it absolutely shies away from looking at the externally sense-perceptible aspect of the world. While the heathen view saw divine spiritual beings everywhere, the god of the Jews is the One God. The Old Testament Jew is a monotheist. His god, Jahve, is the One God, because he can only take account of man as a unity: You must believe in the One God, and you shall not depict this One God in any earthly manner, not in an idol, not even in a word. The name of God may only be spoken by initiates on certain solemn occasions. You must not take the name of your God in vain.

Everything points to what cannot be seen, to what cannot come to expression in nature, to what can only be thought. But behind the thought in the Old Testament there is still the living nature of Jahve. This disappears in the allegories of Philo of Alexandria.

Then came the early Christian struggles—right on into the fifteenth, sixteenth, seventeenth centuries—to reach a harmony between what can be seen as the spirit in external nature and what can be experienced as the divine when we look at our own moral world, our own human soul. In theory the matter seems simple. But in fact the quest for harmony, between seeing the spirit in external nature and guiding the soul upwards to the spiritual world out of which Christ Jesus had descended, was an immense struggle. Christianity came over from Asia and took hold of the Greek and Roman world. In the later centuries of the Middle Ages we see the struggle taking place most strongly in those parts of Europe, which had retained much of their primeval vitality. In ancient Greece the old heathen element was so strong that although Christianity passed through Greek culture and assimilated many Greek expressions on the way, it could not take root there. Only Gnosis, the spiritual view of Christianity, was able to take root in Greece.

Next, Christianity had to pass through the most prosaic element of world evolution: Roman culture. Being abstract, Roman culture could only comprehend the abstract, as it were foreshadowing in an ahrimanic way what is later alive in Christianity. A truly living struggle then took place in Spain. Here, a question was asked which was not theoretical but vital, intensely alive: How can man, without losing sight of the spirit in natural creatures and processes, find the whole human being revealed to him by Christ Jesus. How can man be filled with Christ? This question lived most strongly in Spain, and we see in Calderón[2] a poet who knew how to depict this struggle with great intensity. The struggle to fill the human being with Christ lived—if I may put it like this—dramatically in Calderón.

Calderón's most characteristic drama in this respect is about Cyprianus, a kind of miracle-working magician; in other words he is, in the first instance, a person who lives in natural things and natural processes because he seeks the spirit in them. A later metamorphosis of this character is Faust, but Faust is not as filled with life as is Calderón's Cyprianus. Calderón's portrayal of how Cyprianus stands in the spirit of nature is still filled with life. His attitude is taken absolutely for granted, whereas in the case of Faust everything is shrouded in doubt. From the start, Faust does not really believe that it is possible to find the spirit in nature. But Calderón's Cyprianus is, in this respect, a character who belongs fully to the Middle Ages. A modern physicist or chemist is surrounded in his laboratory by scientific equipment—the physicist by Geissler tubes and other things, the chemist by test tubes, Bunsen burners and the like. Cyprianus, on the other hand, stands with his soul surrounded by the spirit, everywhere flashing out and spilling over from natural processes and natural creatures.

Characteristically, a certain Justina enters into the life of Cyprianus. The drama depicts her quite simply as a woman, but to see her solely as a female human being is not to see the whole of her. These medieval poets are misunderstood by modern interpretations which state that everything simply depicts the material world. They tell us, for instance, that Dante's Beatrice is no more than a gentle female creature. Some interpretations, on the other hand, miss the actual situation by going in the opposite direction, lifting everything up allegorically into a spiritual sphere. But at that time the spiritual pictures and the physical creatures of the earth were not as widely separated as they are in the minds of modern critics today. So when Justina makes her debut in Calderón's drama, we may permit ourselves to think of the element of justice which pervades the whole world. This was not then as abstract as it is now, for now it is found between the covers of tomes which the lawyers can take down from their shelves. Jurisprudence was then felt to be something living.

So Justina comes to Cyprianus. And the hymn about Justina which Cyprianus sings presents another difficulty for modern scientific critics. Modern lawyers do not sing hymns about their jurisprudence, but Cyprianus sensed that the justice which pervades the world was something to which he could sing hymns. We cannot help repeating that spiritual life has changed. Now Cyprianus is at the same time a magician who has dealings with the spirits of nature, that world of demons among whose number the medieval being of Satan can be counted. Cyprianus feels incapable of making a full approach to Justina, so he turns to Satan, the leader of the nature demons, and asks him to win her for him.

Here we have the deep tragedy of the Christian conflict. What approaches Cyprianus in Justina is the justice which is appropriate for Christian development. This justice is to be brought to Cyprianus, who is still a semi-heathen nature scholar. The tragedy is that out of the necessities of nature, which are rigid, he cannot find Christian justice. He can only turn instead to Satan, the leader of the demons, and ask him to win Justina for him.

Satan sets about this task. Human beings find it difficult to understand why Satan—who is, of course, an exceedingly clever being—is ever and again prepared to tackle tasks at which he has repeatedly failed. This is a fact. But however clever we might consider ourselves to be, this is not the way in which to criticize a being as clever as Satan. We should rather ask ourselves what it could be that again and again persuades a being as clever as Satan to try his luck at bringing ruin on human beings. For of course ruin for human beings would have been the result if Satan had succeeded in—let me say—winning over Christian justice in order to bring her to Cyprianus. Well—so Satan sets about his task, but he fails. It is Justina's disposition to feel nothing but revulsion for Satan. She flees from him and he retains only a phantom, a shadow image of her.

You see how various motifs which recur in Faust are to be found in Calderón's drama, but here they are bathed in this early Christian struggle. Satan brings the shadow image to Cyprianus. But Cyprianus does not know what to do with a phantom, a shadow image. It has no life. It bears within it only a shadow image of justice. This drama expresses in a most wonderful way what ancient nature wisdom has become now that it masquerades in the guise of modern science, and how, when it approaches social life—that is, when it approaches Justina—it brings no life with it, but only phantom thoughts. Now, with the fifth post-Atlantean period, mankind has entered upon the age of dead thoughts which gives us only phantoms, phantoms of justice, phantoms of love, phantoms of everything—well, not absolutely everything in life, but certainly in theory.

As a result of all this, Cyprianus goes mad. The real Justina is thrown into prison together with her father. She is condemned to death. Cyprianus hears this in the midst of his madness and demands his own death as well. They meet on the scaffold. Above the scene of their death the serpent appears and, riding on the serpent, the demon who had endeavoured to lead Justina to Cyprianus, declaring that they are saved. They can rise up into the heavenly worlds: 'This noble member of the spirit world is rescued from evil!'

The whole of the Christian struggle of the Middle Ages is contained in this drama. The human being is placed midway between what he is able to experience before birth in the world of spirit and soul, and what he ought to experience after passing through the portal of death. Christ came down to earth because human beings could no longer see what in earlier times they had seen in their middle, rhythmic system which was trained by the breathing exercises of yoga. The middle system was trained, not the head system. These days human beings cannot find the Christ, but they strive to find him. Christ came down. Because they no longer have him in their memory of the time between death and a new birth, human beings must find him here on earth.

Dramas such as the Cyprianus drama of Calderón describe the struggle to find Christ. They describe the difficulties human beings face now that they are supposed to return to the spiritual world and experience themselves in harmony with the spiritual world. Cyprianus is still caught in the demonic echoes of the ancient heathen world. He has also not sufficiently overcome the ancient Hebrew element and brought it down to earth. Jahve is still enthroned in the supersensible worlds, has not descended through the death on the cross, and has not yet become united with the earth. Cyprianus and Justina experience their coming together with the spiritual world as they step through the portal of death—so terrible is the struggle to bring Christ into human nature in the time between birth and death. And there is an awareness that the Middle Ages are not yet mature enough to bring Christ in in this way.

The Spanish drama of Cyprianus shows us the whole vital struggle to bring in the Christ far more vividly than does the theology of the Middle Ages, which strove to remain in abstract concepts and capture the Mystery of Golgotha in abstract terms. In the dramatic and tragic vitality of Calderón there lives the medieval struggle for Christ, that is, the struggle to fill the nature of the human being with the Christ. When we compare Calderón's Cyprianus drama with the later drama about Faust—this is quite characteristic—we find first in Lessing[3] the awareness: Human beings must find the Christ during their earthly life because Christ endured the Mystery of Golgotha and united himself with earthly mankind. Not that this lived in any very clear ideas in Lessing, but he did have a definite sense for it. The fragment of his *Faust* which Lessing succeeded in getting down on paper concludes when the demons—those who were still able to prevent Cyprianus from finding the Christ during earthly life—receive the call: 'You shall not conquer!'

This set the theme for the later *Faust* of Goethe. And even in Goethe the manner in which the human being finds Christianity is rather external. Think of Goethe's *Faust*: In Part One we have the struggle. Then we come to Part Two. In the Classical Walpurgis-Night and in the drama of Helena we are shown first how Christianity is taken up with reference to the Grecian world. Goethe knows that human beings must forge their links with Christ while they are here on the earth. So he must lead his hero to Christianity. But how? I have to say that this is still only a theoretical kind of knowledge—Goethe was too great a poet for us not to notice that this was only a theoretical kind of knowledge. For actually we find that the ascent in the Christian sense only comes in the final act, where it is tacked on to the end of the whole drama. It is certainly all very wonderful, but it does not come out of the inner nature of Faust. Goethe simply took the Catholic dogma. He used the Catholic cultus and simply tacked the fifth act on to the others. He knew that the human being must come to be filled with Christ. Basically the whole mood that lives in the second part of Faust contains this being filled with the Christ. But still Goethe could not find pictures with which to show what should happen. It is really only after Faust's death that the ascent into Christianity is unfolded.

I wanted to mention all this in order to show you how presumptuous it is to speak in a light-hearted way about achieving a consciousness of the Mystery of Golgotha, a consciousness of Christianity. For to achieve a consciousness of Christianity is a task which entails severe struggles of the kind I have mentioned. It behoves mankind today to seek these spiritual forces within the historical evolution of the Middle Ages and modern times. And after the terrible catastrophe we have all been through, human beings really ought to realize how important it is to turn the eye of their souls to these spiritual impulses.

LECTURE TEN

Dornach, 19 February 1922

We have once more pointed out in these lectures that in the most recent cultural period of human evolution, the fifth post-Atlantean period, the main force governing human soul life is the force of the intellect, the force of ideas living in thoughts. To this we had to add the statement that the force of thoughts is actually the corpse of our life of spirit and soul as it was before birth. More and more strongly in recent times this force of thought has emancipated itself from the other forces of the human being, and this was clearly felt by those spirits who wanted to attain a full understanding of the Christian impulse.

Yesterday I endeavoured to describe this, using the example of Calderón's Cyprianus. That drama depicts, on the one hand, the struggles which arise out of the old ideas of a nature filled with soul and, on the other, the strong sense of helplessness encountered by the human being who distances himself from this old view and is forced to seek shelter in mere thoughts. We saw how Cyprianus had to seek the assistance of Satan in order to win Justina—whose significance I endeavoured to explain. But in consequence of the new soul principle, which is now dominant, all he could receive from Satan was a phantom of Justina.

All these things show forcefully how human beings, striving for the spirit, felt in this new age, how they felt the deadness of mere thought life and how, at the same time, they felt that it would be impossible to enter with these mere thoughts into the living realm of the Christ concept. I then went on yesterday to show that the phase depicted in Calderón's Cyprianus drama is followed by another, which we find in Goethe's *Faust*. Goethe is a personality who stands fully in the cultural life of the eighteenth century, which was actually far more international than were later times, and which also had a really strong feeling for the intellectual realm, the realm of thoughts. We can certainly say that in his young days Goethe explored all the different sciences much as did the Faust he depicts in his drama. For in what the intellectual realm had to offer, Goethe did not seek what most people habitually seek; he was searching for a genuine connection with the world to which the eternal nature of man belongs. We can certainly say that Goethe sought true knowledge. But he could not find it through the various sciences at his disposal. Perhaps Goethe approached the figure of Faust in an external way to start with. But because of his own special inclinations he sensed in this Faust figure the struggling human being about whom we spoke yesterday. And in a certain sense he identified with this struggling human being.

Goethe worked on *Faust* in three stages. The first stage leads us back to his early youth when he felt utterly dissatisfied with his university studies and longed to escape from it all and find a true union of soul with the whole of cultural life. Faust was depicted as the struggling human being, the human being striving to escape from mere intellect into a full comprehension of the cosmic origins of man. So this early figure of Faust takes his place beside the other characters simply as the striving human being. Then Goethe underwent those stages of his development during which he submerged himself in the art of the South which he saw as giving form on a higher plane to the essence of nature. He increasingly sought the spirit in nature, for he could not find it in the cultural life that at first presented itself to him. A deep longing led him to the art of the South, which he regarded as the last remnant of Greek art. There, in the way the secrets of nature were depicted artistically out of the Greek world view, he believed he would discover the spirituality of nature.

And then everything he had experienced in Italy underwent a transformation within his soul. We see this transformation given living expression in the intimate form of his fairy-tale[1] about the Green Snake and the Beautiful Lily, in which, out of certain traditional concepts of beauty, wisdom, virtue and strength, he created the temple with the four Kings.

Then, at the end of the eighteenth century, we see how, encouraged by Schiller, he returns to *Faust*, enriched with this world of ideas. This second stage of his work on *Faust* is marked particularly by the appearance of the 'Prologue in Heaven', that wonderful poem which begins with the words: 'The sun makes music as of old, Amid the rival spheres of heaven.'[2] In the drama as Goethe now conceives it, Faust no longer stands there as a solitary figure concerned solely with himself. Now we have the cosmos with all the forces of the universe ascending and descending, and within this cosmos the human being whom the powers of good and evil do battle to possess. Faust takes his place within the cosmos as a whole. Goethe has expanded the material from a question of man alone to a question encompassing the whole of the universe.

The third stage begins in the twenties of the nineteenth century, when Goethe sets about completing the drama. Once again quite new thoughts live in his soul, very different from those with which he was concerned at the end of the eighteenth century when he composed the 'Prologue in Heaven', using ancient ideas about nature, ideas of the spirit in nature, in order to raise the question of Faust to the level of a question of the cosmos. In the twenties, working to bring the second part of the drama to a conclusion, Goethe has returned once more to the human soul out of which he now wants to draw everything, expanding the soul-being once more into a cosmic being.

Of course he has to make use of external representations, but we see how he depicts dramatically the inner journeyings of the soul. Consider the 'Classical Walpurgis-Night' or the reappearance of the Helena scene, which had been there earlier, though merely in the form of an episode. And consider how, in the great final tableau, he endeavours to bring to a concluding climax the soul's inner experience, which is at the same time a cosmic experience when it becomes spiritual. Finally the drama flows over into a Christian element. But, as I said yesterday, this Christian element is not developed out of Faust's experiences of soul but is merely tacked on to the end. Goethe made a study of the Catholic cultus and then tacked this Christianizing element on to the end of *Faust*. There is only an external connection between Faust's inner struggles and the way in which the drama finally leads into this Christian tableau of the universe. This is not intended to belittle the Faust drama. But it has to be said that Goethe, who wrestled in the deepest sense of the word to depict how the spiritual world should be found in earthly life, did not, in fact, succeed in discovering a way of depicting this finding of spirituality in earthly life. To do so, he would have had to come to a full comprehension of the meaning of the Mystery of Golgotha. He would have had to understand how the Christ-being came from the expanses of the cosmos and descended into the human being, Jesus of Nazareth, and how he united himself with the earth, so that ever since then, when seeking the spirit which ebbs and flows in the stormy deeds of man, one ought to find the Christ-impulse in earthly life.

Goethe was never able to make the link between the spirit of the earth, ebbing and flowing in stormy deeds, in the weaving of time, and the Christ-impulse. In a way this may be felt to be a tragedy. But it came about of necessity, because the period of human evolution in which Goethe stood did not yet provide the ground on which the full significance of the Mystery of Golgotha could be comprehended. Indeed, this Mystery of Golgotha can only be fully comprehended if human beings learn to give new life to the dead thoughts which are a part of them in this fifth post-Atlantean period. Today there is a tremendous amount of prejudice, in thought, in feeling and in will, against the re-enlivening of the world of thought. But mankind must solve this problem. Mankind must learn to give new life to this world of thought which enters human nature at birth and conception as the corpse of spirit and soul; this corpse of thoughts and ideas must be made to live again. But this can only happen when thoughts are transformed—first into Imaginations, and then the Imaginations transformed into Inspirations and Intuitions. What is needed is a full understanding of the human being. Not until this becomes a reality, will what I told you yesterday be fully understood: That the world around us must come to be seen as a tremendous question to which the human being himself provides the answer. This is what was to have been given to mankind with the Mystery of Golgotha. It will not be understood until the human being is understood.

Let us look at a diagram of threefold man once more: the human being of the head or of the nerves and senses as discussed yesterday;

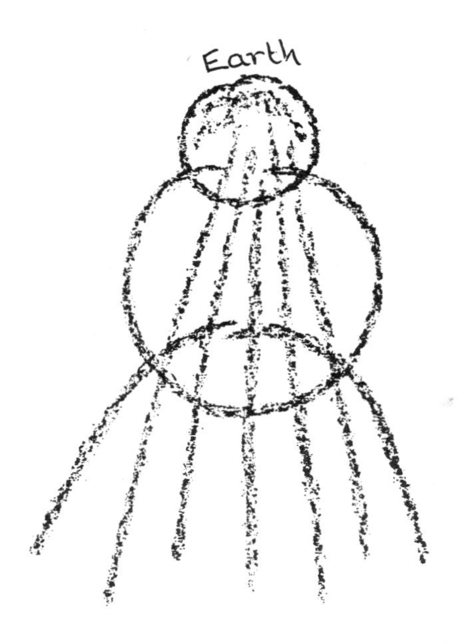

the human being of the rhythmic system or of the chest; and the human being of the metabolism and limbs.

Looking at the human being today, we accept him as the external form in which he appears to us. Someone dissecting a body on the dissecting table has no special feeling that the human head, for instance, is in any way very different from, say, a finger. A finger muscle is considered in the same way as is a muscle in the head. But it ought to be known that the head is, in the main, a metamorphosis of the system of limbs and metabolism from the preceding incarnation; in other words, the head occupies a place in evolution which is quite different from that of the system of limbs that goes with it.

Having at last struggled through to a view of the inner aspect of threefold man, we shall then be in a position to come to a view of what is linked from the cosmos with this threefold human being. As far as our external being is concerned, we are in fact only incarnated in the solid, earthly realm through our head organization. We should never be approachable as a creature of the solid earth if we did not possess our head organization, which is, however, an echo of the limb organization of our previous incarnation. The fact that we have solid parts also in our hands and feet is the result of what rays down from the head. But it is our head which makes us solid. Everything solid and earthly in us derives from our head, as far as the forces in it are concerned.

In our head the solid earth is in us. And whatever is solid anywhere else in our body rays down through us from our head. The origin of our solid bones lies in our head. But there is also in our head a transition to the watery element. All the solid parts of our brain are embedded in the cerebral fluid. In our head there is a constant intermingling vibration of the solid parts of our brain with the cerebral fluid which is linked to the rest of the body by way of the spinal fluid. So, looking at the human being of nerves and senses, we can say that here is the transition from the earthly element (blue) to the watery element. We can say that the human being of nerves and senses lives in the earthy-watery element. And in accordance with this, our brain consists of an intercorrespondence between the earthy and watery elements.

Now let us turn to the chest organism, the rhythmic organism. This rhythmic organism lives in the interrelationship between the watery and the airy element (yellow). In the lungs you can see the watery element making contact with the airy element. The rhythmic life is

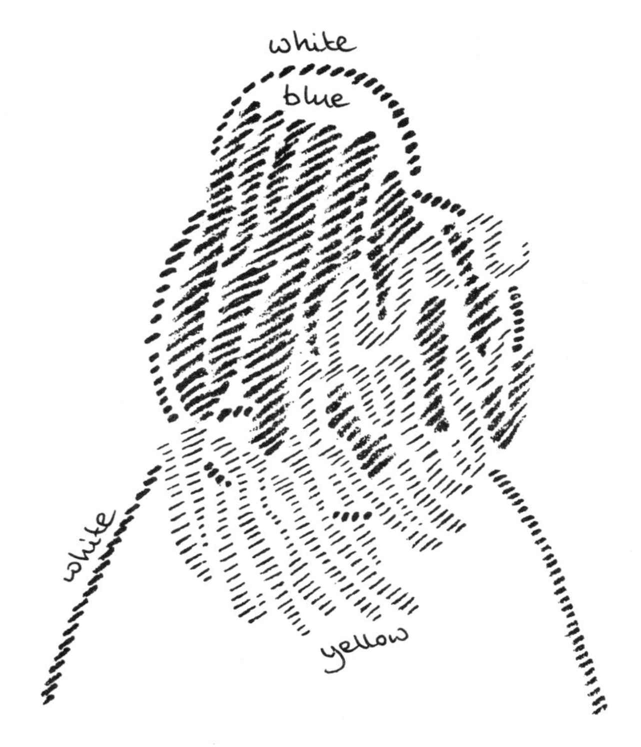

an intermingling of the watery with the airy element, of water with air. So I could say: The rhythmical human being lives in the watery-airy element.

And the human being of metabolism and limbs then lives in the transition from the airy element to the warmth element, in the fiery element (red, p. 114). It is a constant dissolving of the airy element in the warmth, the fiery element, which then seeps through the whole human being as his body heat. What happens in our metabolism and in our movements is a reorganization of the airy, gaseous element up into the warm, fiery element. As we move about, we constantly burn up those elements of the food we have eaten which have become airy. Even when we do not move about, the foods we eat are transformed into airy elements which we constantly burn up in the warmth element.

So the human being of limbs and metabolism lives in the airy-fiery element.

Human being of nerves and senses:	earthy-watery element
Rhythmical human being:	watery-airy element
Human being of limbs and metabolism:	airy-fiery element

From here we go up even further into the etheric parts, into the light element, into the etheric body of the human being. When the organism of metabolism and limbs has transferred everything into warmth, it then goes up into the etheric body. Here the human being joins up with the etheric realm which fills the whole world; here he makes the link with the cosmos.

Ideas like this, which I have shown you only as diagrams, can be transformed into artistic and poetic form by someone who has an inner sense for sculpture and music. In a work of poetry such as the drama of *Faust* such things can certainly be expressed in artistic form, in the way certain cosmic secrets are expressed, for instance, in the seventh scene of my first Mystery Drama.[3] This leads to the possibility of seeing the human being linked once more with the cosmos. But for this we cannot apply to the human being what our intellect teaches us about external nature. You must understand that if you study external nature, and then study your head in the same way as you would external nature, you are then studying something which simply does not belong to external nature as it now is, but something that comes from your former incarnation. You are studying something as though it had arisen at the present moment; but it is not something that has arisen out of the present moment, nor could it ever arise out of the present moment. For a human head could not possibly arise out of the forces of nature which exist. So the human head must not be studied in the same way as objects are studied with the intellect. It must be studied with the knowledge given by Imagination. The human head will not be understood until it is studied with the knowledge given by Imagination.

In the rhythmical human being everything comes into movement. Here we have to do with the watery and the airy elements. Everything

is in surging movement. The external, solid parts of our breast organization are only what our head sends down into this surging motion. To study the rhythmical human being we have to say that in this rhythmical surging the watery element and the airy element mingle together (see diagram, green, yellow). Into this, the head sends the possibility for the solid parts, such as those in the lungs, to be present (white). This surging, which is the real rhythmical human being, can only be studied with the knowledge given by Inspiration. So the rhythmical human being can only be studied with the knowledge given by Inspiration.

And the human being of limbs and metabolism—this is the continuous burning of the air in us. You stand within it, in your warmth you feel yourself to be a human being, but this is a very obscure idea. It can only be studied properly with the knowledge given by Intuition, in which the soul stands within the object. Only the knowledge given by Intuition can lead to the human being of metabolism and limbs.

The human being will remain forever unknown if he is not studied with the knowledge given by Imagination, Inspiration and Intuition. He will forever remain the external shell which is all that is recognized today, both in general and in science. This situation must not be allowed to remain. The human being must come once more to be recognized for what he is. If you study only the solid parts of the human being, the parts which are shown in the illustrations in anatomy textbooks, then, right from the start, you are studying wrongly. Your study ought to be in the realm of Imagination, because all these illustrations of the solid parts of the human organism ought to be taken as images brought over from the previous incarnation. This is the first thing. Then come the even more delicate parts which live in the physical constituents. These can only be studied with the knowledge given by Inspiration. And the airy-watery element can only be studied with the knowledge given by Intuition. These things must be taken into European consciousness, indeed into the whole of modern civilization. If we fail to place them in the mainstream of culture, our civilization will only go downhill instead of upwards.

When you understand what Goethe intended with his *Faust*, you sense that he was endeavouring to pass through a certain gateway. Everywhere he is struggling with the question: What is it that we need to know about this human being? As a very young man he began to study the human form. Read his discourse on the intermaxillary bone and also what I wrote about it in my edition of his scientific writings.[4] He is endeavouring so hard to come to an understanding of man. First he tried by way of anatomy and physiology. Then in the nineties he explored the aspect of moral ideas which we find in the fairy tale of the Green Snake and the Beautiful Lily. Then, in *Faust*, he wants to depict the human being as he stands in the world. He is trying to pass through a gateway in order to discover how the human being does, in fact, stand in the world. But he lacks the necessary prerequisites; he cannot do it.

When Calderón wrote his drama about Cyprianus, the struggle was still taking place at a previous level. We see how Justina tears herself free of Satan's clutches, how Cyprianus goes mad, how they find one another in death, and how their salvation comes as they meet their end on the scaffold. Above them the serpent appears—on it rides the demon who is forced to announce their salvation.

We see that at the time when Calderón was writing his Cyprianus drama the message to be clearly stated was: You cannot find the divine, spiritual realm here on earth. First you must die and go through the portal of death; then you will discover the divine spiritual world, that salvation which you can find through Christ. They were still far from understanding the Mystery of Golgotha through which Christ had descended to earth, where it now ought to be possible to find him. Calderón still has too many heathen and Jewish elements in his ideas for him to have a fully developed sense for Christianity.

After that, a good deal of time passed before Goethe started to work on his *Faust*. He sensed that it was necessary for Faust to find his salvation here on earth. The question he should therefore have asked was: How can Faust discover the truth of Paul's words: 'Not I, but Christ in me'?[5] Goethe should have let his Faust say not only, to 'Stand on free soil among a people free',[6] but also: to 'stand on free soil with Christ in one's soul leading the human being in earthly life to the spirit'. Goethe should have let Faust say something like this. But Goethe is honest; he does not say it because he has not yet fully understood it. But he is striving to understand it. He is striving for something which can only be achieved when it is possible to say: Learn to know man through Imagination, Inspiration, Intuition. That he is striving in this way gives us the feeling that there is much more in his struggle and in his endeavour than he ever managed to express or than has filtered through into today's culture. Perhaps he can only be fully recognized by doing what I did in my early writings when I endeavoured to express the world view which lived almost unconsciously in him. However, on the whole, his search has met with little understanding amongst the people of today.

When I look at this whole situation in connection with modern civilization, I am constantly reminded of my old teacher and friend, Karl Julius Schröer.[7] I think particularly of how, in the eighties of the last century, Schröer was working on *Faust* and on Goethe's other plays, writing commentaries, introductions and so on. He was not in the least concerned to speak about Goethe in clearly defined concepts but merely gave general indications. Yet he was at pains to make people understand that what lived most profoundly in Goethe must enter into mainstream modern culture. On the fiftieth anniversary of Goethe's death, in 1882, Schröer gave an address: 'How the future will see Goethe'. He lived with the dream that the time had already come for a kind of resurrection of Goethe. Then we wrote a short essay in *Die Neue Freie Presse* which was reprinted in the booklet 'Goethe and Love'. This and other of his writings have now been acquired by our publisher, *Der Kommende Tag*, so remaindered copies can be acquired there, and there will also be new editions eventually. This essay 'Goethe after 50 Years' is a brief extract from that lecture, at which I was present. It contains a good deal of what Schröer felt at that time regarding the need for Goethe to be assimilated into modern culture. And then in this booklet 'Goethe and Love' he endeavoured to show in the notes how Goethe could be made to come alive, for to bring Goethe to life is, in a sense, to bring the world of abstract thoughts to life. In the recent number of *Das Goetheanum* I referred to a beautiful passage about this in the booklet 'Goethe and Love'. Schröer says: 'Schiller recognized him. When an intuitive genius searches for the character of necessity in the empirical realm, he will always produce individuals even though these may have a generic aspect. With his intuitive method of seeing the eternal idea, the primeval type, in the mortal individual, Goethe is perhaps not as alone as one might assume.'

While Schröer was writing this booklet in 1882 I visited him a number of times. He was filled to the brim with an impression he had had. He had heard somewhere how Oppolzer, a physician in Vienna, used a rather vague intuitive faculty when making his diagnoses. Instead of examining the patient in the usual way, he allowed the type of the patient to make an impression on him, and from the type of the patient he deduced something of the type of the illness. This made a strong impression on Schröer, and he used this phenomenon to enlarge on what he was trying to explain: 'In medicine we extol the ability of great diagnosticians to fathom the disease by intuitively discerning the individual patient's type, his habitude. They are not helped by chemical or anatomical knowledge but by an intuitive sense for the living creature as a whole being. They are creative spirits who see the sun because their eye is sunlike. Others do not see the sun. What these diagnosticians are doing unconsciously is to follow the intuitive method which Goethe consciously applied as a means of scientific study. The results he achieved are no longer disputed, though the method is not yet generally recognized.'

Out of a conspectus which included Oppolzer's intuitive bedside method, Schröer even then was pointing out that the different sciences, for example, medicine, needed fructifying by a method which worked together with the spirit.

It is rather tragic to look back and see in Schröer one of the last of those who still sensed what was most profound in Goethe. At the beginning of the eighties of the last century Schröer believed that there would have to be a Goethe revival, but soon after that Goethe was truly nailed into his coffin and buried with sweeping finality. His grave, we could say, was in Central Europe, in the *Goethe-Gesellschaft*, whose English branch was called the Goethe Society. This is where the living Goethe was buried. But now it is necessary to bring this living element, which was in Goethe, back into our culture. Karl Julius Schröer's instinct was good. In his day he was unable to fulfil it because his contemporaries continued to worship the dead Goethe. 'He who would study organic existence, first drives out the soul with rigid persistence.'[8]

This became the motto, and in some very wide circles this motto has intensified into a hatred against any talk of spiritual things—as you can see in the way Anthroposophy is received by many people.

Today's culture, which all of you have as your background, urgently needs this element of revival. It is quite extraordinary how much talk there is today of Goethe's *Faust*, which after all simply represents a new stage in the struggle for the spirit which we saw in Calderón's Cyprianus drama. So much is said about *Faust*, yet there is no understanding for the task of the present time, which is to bring fully to life what Goethe brought to life in his *Faust*, especially in the second part. Goethe brought it to life in a vague, intuitive sensing, though not with full spiritual insight. We ought to turn our full attention to this, for indeed it is not only a matter of a world view. It is a matter of our whole culture and civilization. There are many symptoms, if only we can see them in the right light.

Here is an essay by Ruedorffer[9] entitled 'The Three Crises'.

Every page gives us a painful knock. The writer played important roles in the diplomatic and political life of Europe before the war and on into the war. Now, with his intimate knowledge of the highways and byways of European life, and because he was able to observe things from vantage points not open to most, he is seeking an explanation of what is actually going on. I need only read you a few passages. He wants to be a realist, not an idealist. During the course of his diplomatic career he has developed a sober view of life. And despite the fact that he has written such things as the passages I am going to read to you he remains that much appreciated character, a bourgeois philistine.

He deals with three things in his essay. Firstly he says that the countries and nations of Europe no longer have any relationship with one another. Then he says that the governing circles, the leaders of the different nations, have no relationship with the population. And thirdly he says that those people in particular who want to work out and found a new age by radical means most certainly have no relationship with reality.

So a person who played his part in bringing about the situation that now exists writes: 'This sickness of the state organism snatches leadership away from good sense and hands responsibility for decisions of state to all sorts of minor influences and secondary considerations. It inhibits freedom of movement, fragments the national will and usually also leads to a dangerous instability of governments. The period of unruly nationalism that preceded the war, the war itself, and the situation in Europe since the war, have made monstrous demands on the good sense of all the states, and on their peace and their freedom to manoevre. The loss of wealth brought about by necessary measures has completed the catastrophe. The crisis of the state and the crisis in world-wide organization have mutually exacerbated the situation, each magnifying the destructive effect of the other.' These are not the words of an idealist, or of some artistic spirit who watched from the sidelines, but of someone who shared in creating the situation. He says, for instance: 'If democracy is to endure, it must be honest and courageous enough to call a spade a spade, even if it means bearing witness against itself. Europe faces ruin.'

So it is not only pessimistic idealists who say that Europe is faced with ruin. The same is said especially by those who stood in the midst of practical life. One of these very people says:

'Europe faces ruin. There is no time to waste by covering up mistakes for party political reasons, instead of setting about putting them to rights. It is for this reason alone, and not to set myself up as *laudator temporis acti*, that I have to stress that democracy must, and will, destroy itself if it cannot free the state from this snare of minor influences and secondary considerations. Pre-war Europe collapsed because all the countries of the continent—the monarchies as well as the democracies and, above all, autocratic Russia—succumbed to demagogy, partly voluntarily, partly unconsciously, partly with reluctance because their hand was forced. In the confusion of mind, for which they had only themselves to thank, they were incapable of recognizing good sense, and even if they had recognized it they would have been incapable of acting on it freely and decisively. The higher social strata of the old states of Europe—who, in the last century, were certainly the bearers of European culture and rich in personalities of statesmanlike quality and much world experience—would not have been so easily thrown from the saddle, rotten and expended, if they had grown with the problems and tasks of new times, if they had not lost their statesmanlike spirit, and if they had preserved any more worthwhile tradition than that of the most trivial diplomatic routine. If monarchs claim the ability to select statesmen more proficiently and expertly than governments, then they and their courts must be the centre and epitome of culture, insight and understanding. Long before the war this ceased to be the case. But indictment of the monarchs' failures does not exonerate the democracies from recognizing the causes of their own inadequacies or from doing everything possible to eliminate them. Before Europe can recover, before any attempt can be made to replace its hopeless disorganization with a durable political structure, the individual countries will have to tidy up their internal affairs to an extent which will free their governments for long-term serious work. Otherwise, the best will in the world and the greatest capability will be paralysed, tied down by the web of the disaster which is the same wherever we look.'

I would not bother to read all this to you if it had been written by an idealist, instead of by someone who considers his feet to be firmly on the ground of reality because he played a part in bringing the current situation about.

'The drama is deeply tragic. Every attempt at improvement, every word of change, becomes entangled in this web, throttled by a thousand threads, until it falls to the ground without effect. The citizens of Europe—thoughtlessly clutching the contemporary erroneous belief in the constant progress of mankind, or, with loud lamentations trotting along in the same old rut—fail to see, and do not want to see, that they are living off the stored-up labour of earlier years; they are barely capable of recognizing the present broken-down state of the world order, and are certainly incapable of bringing a new one to birth. On the other hand, the workers, treading a radical path in almost every country and convinced of the untenability of the present situation, believe themselves to be the bringers of salvation through a new order of things; but in reality this belief has made them into nothing more than an unconscious tool of destruction and decline, their own included. The new parasites of economic disorganization, the complaining rich of yester-year, the *petit bourgeois* descending to the level of the proletariat, the gullible worker believing himself to be the founder of a new world—all of them seem to be engulfed by the same disaster, all of them are blind men digging their own grave.'

Remember, this is not written by an idealist, but by one who shared in bringing about this situation!

'But every political factor today—the recent peace treaties of the *Entente*, the Polish invasion of the Ukraine, the blindness or helplessness of the *Entente* with regard to developments in Germany and Austria—proves to the politician who depends on reality that although idealistic demands for a pan-European, constructive revision of the Paris peace treaties can be made, although the most urgent warnings can be shockingly justified, nevertheless, both demands and warnings can but die away unnoticed while everything rolls on unchanged towards the inevitable end—the abyss.'

The whole book is written in order to prove that Europe has come to the brink of the abyss and that we are currently employed in digging the grave of European civilization. But all this is only an introduction to what I now find it necessary to say to you. What I have to say is something different. Here we have a man who was himself an occupant of crucial seats of office, a man who realizes that Europe is on the brink of the abyss. And yet—as we can see in the whole of his book—all he has to say is: If all that happens is only a continuation of older impulses, then civilization will perish; it will definitely perish. Something new must come.

So now let me search for this new thing to which he wants to point. Yes, here it is, on page 67; here it is, in three lines: 'Only a change of heart in the world, a change of will by the major powers, can lead to the creation of a supreme council of European good sense.'

Yes, this is the decision that faces these people. They point out that only if a change of heart comes about, if something entirely new is brought into being, can the situation be saved. This whole book is written to show that without this there can be no salvation. There is a good deal of truth in this. For, in truth, salvation for our collapsing civilization can only come from a spiritual life drawn from the real sources of the spirit. There is no other salvation. Without it, modern civilization, in so far as it is founded in Europe and reaches across to America, is drawing towards its close. Decay is the most important phenomenon of our time. There is no help in reaching compromises with decay. Help can only come from turning to something that can flourish above the grave, because it is more powerful than death. And that is spiritual life. But people like the writer of this book have only the most abstract notion of what this entails. They say an international change of heart must take place. If anything is said about a real, new blossoming of spiritual life, this is branded as 'useless mysticism'. All people can say is: Look at them, bringing up all kinds of occult and mystical things; we must have nothing to do with them.

Those who are digging the grave of modern civilization most busily are those who actually have the insight to see that the digging is going on. But the only real way of taking up a stance with regard to these things is to look at them squarely, with great earnestness—to meditate earnestly on the fact that a new spiritual life is what is needed and that it is necessary to search for this spiritual life, so that at last a way may be found of finding Christ within earthly life, and of finding Him as He has become since the Mystery of Golgotha. For He descended in order to unite with the conditions of the earth.

The strongest battle against real Christian truth is being fought today by a certain kind of theology which raises its hands in horror at any mention of the cosmic Christ. It is necessary to be reminded again and again that even in the days when Schröer was pointing to Goethe as a source for a regeneration of civilization, a book appeared by a professor in Basel—a friend of Nietzsche—about modern Christian theology. Overbeck[10] considered at that time that theology was the most un-Christian thing, and as a historian of theology he sought to prove this. So there was at that time in Basel a professor of theological history who set out to prove that theology is un-Christian!

Mankind has drifted inevitably towards catastrophe because it failed to hear the isolated calls, which did exist but which were, it must be said, still very unclear. Today there is no longer any time to lose.

Today mankind must know that descriptions such as that given by Ruedorffer are most definitely true and that it is most definitely necessary to realize how everything is collapsing because of the continuation of the old impulses. There is only one course to follow: We must turn towards what can grow out of the grave, out of the living spirit.

This is what must be pointed out ever and again, especially in connection with the things with which we are concerned.

LECTURE ELEVEN

Dornach, 24 February 1922

The turning-point, between the fourth and fifth post-Atlantean periods,[1] which falls in the fifteenth century, is very much more significant for human evolution than is recognized by external history, even today. There is no awareness of the tremendous change which took place at that time in the condition of human souls. We can say that profound traces of what took place at that time for mankind as a whole became deeply embedded in the consciousness of the best spirits. These traces remained for a long time and are indeed still there today. That something so important can take place without at first being much noticed externally is shown by another example—that of Christianity itself.

During the course of almost two thousand years, Christianity has wrought tremendous transformation on the civilized world. Yet, a century after the Mystery of Golgotha, it meant little, even to the greatest spirits of the leading culture of the time—that of Rome. It was still seen as a minor event of little significance that had taken place out there in Asia, on the periphery of the Empire. Similarly, what took place in the civilized world around the first third of the fifteenth century has been little noted in external, recorded history. Yet it has left deep traces in human striving and endeavour.

We spoke about some aspects recently. For instance, we saw that Calderón's[2] drama about the magician Cyprianus shows how this spiritual change was experienced in Spain. Now it is becoming obvious—though it is not expressed in the way Anthroposophy has to express it—that in all sorts of places at this point in human evolution there is a more vital sense for the need to gain greater clarity of soul about this change. I have also pointed out that Goethe's *Faust* is one of the endeavours, one of the human struggles, to gain clarity about it. More light can perhaps be thrown on this Faust of Goethe when it is seen in a wider cultural context. But first let us look at Faust himself as an isolated individual.

First of all in his youthful endeavours, stimulated of course by the cultural situation in Europe at that time, Goethe came to depict in dramatic form the striving of human beings in the newly dawning age of the intellect. From the way in which he came across the medieval Faust figure in a popular play or something similar, he came to see him as a representative of all those seeking personalities who lived at that time. Faust belongs to the sixteenth, not the fifteenth century,[3] but of course the spiritual change did not take place in the space of only a year or even a century. It came about gradually over centuries. So the Faust figure came towards Goethe like a personality living in the midst of this seeking and striving that had come from earlier times and would go on into later centuries. We can see that the special nature of this seeking and striving, as it changed from the fourth to the fifth post-Atlantean period, is perfectly clear to Goethe. First he presents Faust as the scholar who is familiar with all four academic faculties. All four faculties have worked on his soul, so that he has taken into his soul the impulses which derive from intellectualism, from intellectualistic science. At the same time he senses how unsatisfying it is for human beings to remain stuck in one-sided intellectualism. As you know, Faust turns away from this intellectualism and, in his own way, towards the practice of magic. Let us be clear about what is meant in this case. What he has gone through by way of 'Philosophy and Jurisprudence, Medicine and even, alas, Theology,'[4] is what anyone can go through by studying the intellectualized sciences. It leaves a feeling of dissatisfaction. It leaves behind this feeling of dissatisfaction because anything abstract—and abstraction is the language of these sciences—makes demands only on a part of the human being, the head part, while all the rest is left out of account.

Compare this with what it was like in earlier times. The fact that things were different in earlier times is habitually overlooked. In those earlier times the people who wanted to push forward to a knowledge of life and the world did not turn to intellectual concepts. All their efforts were concentrated on seeing spiritual realities, spiritual beings, behind the sense-perceptible objects of their environment. This is what people find so difficult to understand. In the tenth, eleventh, twelfth centuries those who strove for knowledge did not only seek intellectual concepts, they sought spiritual beings and realities, in accordance with what can be perceived behind sense-perceptible phenomena and not in accordance with what can be merely thought about sense-perceptible phenomena.

This is what constitutes that great spiritual change. What people sought in earlier times was banished to the realm of superstition, and the inclination to seek for real spiritual beings was lost. Instead, intellectual concepts came to be the only acceptable thing, the only really scientific knowledge. But no matter how logically people told themselves that the only concepts and ideas free of any superstition are those which the intellect forms on the basis of sense-perceptible reality, nevertheless these concepts and ideas failed, in the long run, to satisfy the human being as a whole, and especially the human heart and soul. In this way Goethe's Faust finds himself to be so dissatisfied with the intellectual knowledge he possesses that he turns back to what he remembers of the realm of magic.

This was a true and genuine mood of soul in Goethe. He, too, had explored the sciences at the University of Leipzig. Turning away from the intellectualism he met in Leipzig, he started to explore what in *Faust* he later called 'magic', for instance, together with Susanne von Klettenberg and also by studying the relevant books. Not until he met Herder[5] in Strasbourg did he discover a real deepening of vision. In him he found a spirit who was equally averse to intellectualism. Herder was certainly not an intellectual; hence his anti-Kant attitude. He led Goethe beyond what—in a genuinely Faustian mood—he had been endeavouring to discover in connection with ancient magic.

Thus Goethe looked at this Faust of the sixteenth century, or rather at that scholar of the fifteenth century who was growing beyond magic, even though he was still half-immersed in it. Goethe wanted to depict his own deepest inner search, a search which was in him because the traces of the spiritual change from the fourth to the fifth post-Atlantean period were still working in him.

It is one of the most interesting phenomena of recent cultural evolution that Goethe, who wanted to give expression to his own youthful striving, should turn to that professor from the fifteenth and sixteenth century. In the figure of this professor he depicted his own inner soul life and experience. Du Bois-Reymond,[6] of course, totally misunderstood both what lived in Goethe and what lived in the great change that took place in the fifteenth and sixteenth centuries, when he said: Goethe made a big mistake in depicting Faust as he did; he should have done it quite differently. It is right that Faust should be dissatisfied with what tradition had to offer him; but if Goethe had depicted him properly he would have shown, after the early scenes, how he first made an honest woman of Gretchen by marrying her, and then became a well-known professor who went on to invent the electro-static machine and the air pump. This is what Du Bois-Reymond thought should have become of Faust.

Well, Goethe did not let this happen to Faust, and I am not sure whether it would have been any more interesting if he had done what Du Bois-Reymond thought he should have done. But as it is, Goethe's Faust is one of the most interesting phenomena of recent cultural history because Goethe felt the urge to let this professor from the fifteenth and sixteenth centuries stand as the representative of what still vibrated in his own being as an echo of that spiritual change which came about during the transition from the fourth to the fifth post-Atlantean period.

The sixteenth century Faust—that is the legendary Faust, not the one who ought to have become the inventor of the electro-static machine and the air pump—takes up magic and perishes, goes to the devil. We know that this sixteenth century Faust could not be seen by either Lessing or Goethe as the Faust of the eighteenth century. Now it was necessary to endeavour to show that once again there was a striving for the spirit and that man ought to find his way to salvation, if I may use this expression.

Here, to begin with, is Faust, the professor in the fifteenth and sixteenth centuries. Goethe has depicted him strikingly well, for this is just what such personalities were like at the universities of that time. Of course, the Faust of legend would not have been suitable, for he would have been more like a roaming vagabond gipsy. Goethe is describing not the legendary Faust but the figure of a professor. Of course, at the profoundest soul level he is an individual, a unique personality. But Goethe does also depict him as a type, as a typical professor of philosophy, or perhaps of medicine, of the fourteenth or fifteenth century. On the one hand he stands in the midst of the culture of his day, occupying himself with the intellectual sciences, but on the other he is not unfamiliar with occult things, which in Goethe's own day were considered nothing more than superstition.

Let us now look at Goethe's Faust in a wider world context. We do make the acquaintance of his famulus and Goethe shows us the relationship between the two. We also meet a student—though judging by his later development he does not seem to have been much influenced by his professor. But apart from this, Goethe does not show us much of the real influence exercised by Faust, in his deeper soul aspects, as he might have taught as a professor in, say, Wittenberg. However, there does exist a pupil of Faust who can lead us more profoundly into this wider world context. There is a pupil of Faust who occupies a place in the cultural history of mankind which is almost equal to that of Professor Faust himself—I am speaking only of Faust as Goethe portrayed him. And this pupil is none other than Hamlet.

Hamlet can indeed be seen as a genuine pupil of Faust. It is not a question of the historical aspect of Faust as depicted by Goethe. The whole action of the drama shows that although the cultural attitudes are those of the eighteenth century, nevertheless Goethe's endeavour was to place Faust in an earlier age. But from a certain point of view it is definitely possible to say: Hamlet, who has studied at Wittenberg and has brought home with him a certain mood of spirit—Hamlet as depicted by Shakespeare,[7] can be seen in the context of world spiritual history as a pupil of Faust. It may even be true to say that Hamlet is a far more genuine pupil of Faust than are the students depicted in Goethe's drama.

Consider the whole character of Hamlet and combine this with the fact that he studied in Wittenberg where he could easily have heard a professor such as Faust. Consider the manner in which he is given his task. His father's ghost appears to him. He is in contact with the real spiritual world. He is really within it. But he has studied in Wittenberg where he was such a good student that he has come to regard the human brain as a book. You remember the scene when Hamlet speaks of the 'book and volume' of his brain.[8] He has studied human sciences so thoroughly that he speaks of writing what he wants to remember on the table of his memory, almost as though he had known the phrase which Goethe would use later when composing his Faust drama: 'For what one has, in black and white, one carries home and then goes through it.'[9] Hamlet is on the one hand an excellent student of the intellectualism taught him at Wittenberg, but on the other hand he is immersed in a spiritual reality. Both impulses work in his soul. The whole of the Hamlet drama stands under the influence of these two impulses. Hamlet—both the drama and the character—stands under the influence of these impulses because, when it comes down to it, the writer of *Hamlet* does not really know how to combine the spiritual world with the intellectual mood of soul. Poetic works which contain characteristics that are so deeply rooted in life provide rich opportunities for discussion. That is why so many books are written about such works, books which do not really make much sense because there is no need for them to make sense. The commentators are constantly concerned with what they consider to be a most important question: Is the ghost in *Hamlet* merely a picture, or does it have objective significance? What can be concluded from the fact that only Hamlet, and not the others characters present on the stage, can see the ghost?

Think of all the learned and interesting things that have been written about this! But of course none of it is connected with what concerned the poet who wrote *Hamlet*. He belonged to the sixteenth and seventeenth centuries. And writing out of the life of that time he could do no other than approach these things in a way which cannot be fixed in abstract concepts. That is why I say that it is not necessary to make any sense of all the various commentaries. We are talking about a time of transition. Earlier, it was quite clear that spiritual beings were as real as tables and chairs, or as a dog or a cat. Although Calderón lived even later than Shakespeare, he still held to this older view. It would not have occurred to him even to hint that the spiritual beings in his works might be merely subjective in character. Because his whole soul was still open to spiritual insight, he portrayed anything spiritual as something just as concrete as dogs and cats.

Shakespeare, whose mood of soul belonged fully to the time of transition, did not feel the need to handle the matter in any other way than that which stated: It might be *like this* or it might be *like that*. There is no longer a clear distinction between whether the spiritual beings are subjective or objective. This is a question which is just as irrelevant for a higher world view as it would be to ask in real life—not in astronomy, of course—where to draw the line between day and night. The question as to whether one is subjective and the other objective becomes irrelevant as soon as we recognize the objectivity of the inner world of man and the subjectivity of the external world. In *Hamlet* and also, say, in *Macbeth*, Shakespeare maintains a living suspension between the two. So we see that Shakespeare's dramas are drawn from the transition between the fourth and fifth post-Atlantean periods.

The expression of this is clearest in *Hamlet*. It may not be historical but it is none the less true to suggest that perhaps Hamlet was at Wittenberg just at the time when Faust was lecturing not so much about the occult as about the intellectual sciences—from what we said earlier you now know what I mean. Perhaps he was at Wittenberg before Faust admitted to himself that, 'straight or crosswise, wrong or right', he had been leading his scholars by the nose these ten years long. Perhaps Hamlet had been at Wittenberg during those very ten years, among those whom Faust had been leading by the nose. We can be sure that during those ten years Faust was not sure of where he stood. So having taken all this in from a soul that was itself uncertain, Hamlet returns and is faced on the one hand with what remains from an earlier age and what he himself can still perceive, and on the other with a human attitude which simply drives the spirits away. Just as ghosts flee before the light, so does the perception of spiritual beings flee before intellectualism. Spiritual vision cannot tolerate intellectualism because the outcome of it is a mood of soul in which the human being is inwardly torn right away from any connection with the spirit. The pallor of thoughts makes him ill in his inner being, and the consequence of this is the soul mood characteristic of the time from the eleventh to the fifteenth centuries and on into even later times. Goethe, who was sensitive to all these things, also had a mood of soul that reached back into this period. We ought to be clear about this.

Take Greek drama. It is unthinkable without the spiritual beings who stand behind it. It is they who determine human destinies. Human beings are woven into the fabric of destiny by the spiritual forces. This fabric brings into ordinary life what human beings would otherwise only experience if they were able consciously to go into the state of sleep. The will impulses which human beings sleep through in their daytime consciousness are brought into ordinary life. Greek destiny is an insight into what man otherwise sleeps through. When the ancient Greek brings his will to bear, when he acts, he is aware that this is not only the working of his daytime consciousness with its insipid thoughts. Because his whole being is at work, he knows that what pulses through him when he sleeps is also at work. And out of this awareness he gains a certain definite attitude to the question of death, the question of immortality.

Now we come to the period I have been describing, in which human beings no longer had any awareness that something spiritual played in—also in their will—while they slept. We come to the period in which human beings thought their sleep was their own, though at the same time they knew from tradition that they have some connection with the spiritual world. Abstract concepts such as 'Philosophy, Jurisprudence, Medicine, and even, alas! Theology' begin to take on a shadowy outline of what they will become in modern times. They begin to appear, but at the same time the earlier vision still plays in. This brings about a twilight consciousness. People really did live in this twilight consciousness. Such figures as Faust are, indeed, born out of a twilight consciousness, out of a glance into the spiritual world which resembles a looking over one's shoulder in a dream. Think of the mood behind such words as 'sleep', or 'dream', in *Hamlet*.

We can well say that when Hamlet speaks his monologues he is simply speaking about what he senses to be the riddle of his age; he is speaking not theoretically but out of what he actually senses.

So, spanning the centuries and yet connected in spirit, we see that Shakespeare depicts the student and Goethe the professor. Goethe depicted the professor simply because a few more centuries had passed and it was therefore necessary in his time to go further back to the source of what it was all about. Something lived in the consciousness of human beings, something that made the outstanding spirits say: I must bring to expression this state of transition that exists in human evolution.

It is extremely interesting to expand on this world situation still further, because out of it there arise a multitude of all-embracing questions and riddles about life and the world. It is interesting to note, for instance, that amongst the works of Shakespeare *Hamlet* is the one which depicts in its purest form a personality belonging to the whole twilight condition of the transition—especially in the monologues. The way Hamlet was understood in the seventeenth and eighteenth centuries could have led to the question: Where was the stimulus for what exists in Hamlet's soul? The answer points to Wittenberg, the Faust source. Similar questions arise in connection with *Macbeth*. But in *King Lear* we move into the human realm. The question of the spiritual world is not so much concerned with the earth as with the human being—it enters into the human being and becomes a subjective state of mind which leads to madness.

Then Shakespeare's other dramas could also be considered. We could say: What the poet learnt by taking these human characters and leading them to the spiritual realm lives on in the historical dramas about the kings. He does not follow this specific theme in the historical dramas, but the indeterminate forces work on. Taking Shakespeare's dramas all together, one gains the impression that they all culminate in the age of Queen Elizabeth. Shakespeare wanted to depict something that leads from the subconscious, bubbling forces of his people to the intellectual clarity that has especially shone forth from that corner of the civilized world since the age of Elizabeth. From this point of view the whole world of Shakespeare's dramas appears—not perhaps quite like a play with a satisfactory ending, but at least like a drama which does lead to a fairly satisfying conclusion. That is, it leads to a world which then continues to evolve. After the transition had been going on for some time, the dramas lead to

Shakespeare's immediate present, which is a world with which it is possible to come to terms. This is the remarkable thing: The world of Shakespeare's dramas culminates in the age in which Shakespeare lived; this is an age with which it is possible to come to terms, because from then on history takes a satisfactory course and runs on into intellectualism. Intellectualism came from the part of the earth out of which Shakespeare wrote; and he depicted this by ending up at this point.

The questions with which I am concerned find their answers when we follow the lines which lead from the pupil Hamlet to the professor Faust, and then ask how it was with Goethe at the time when, out of his inner struggles, he came to the figure of Faust. You see, he also wrote *Götz von Berlichingen*. In *Götz von Berlichingen*, again taken from folk myth, there is a similar confrontation. On the one side you have the old forces of the pre-intellectual age, the old German empire, which cannot be compared with what became the later German empire. You have the knights and the peasants belonging to the pre-intellectual age when the pallor of thoughts did not make human beings ill; when indeed very little was guided from the head, but when the hands were used to such an extent that even an iron hand was needed. Goethe refers back to something that once lived in more recent civilization but which, by its very nature, had its roots in the fourth post-Atlantean period. Over against all this you have in the figure of Weislingen the new element which is developing, the age of intellectualism, which is intimately linked to the way the German princes and their principalities evolved, a development which led eventually to the later situation in Central Europe right up to the present catastrophe.

We see that in *Götz von Berlichingen* Goethe is attacking this system of princes and looking back to times which preceded the age of intellectualism. He takes the side of the old and rebels against what has taken its place, especially in Central Europe. It is as though Goethe were saying in *Götz von Berlichingen* that intellectualism has seized hold of Central Europe too. But here it appears as something that is out of place. It would not have occurred to Goethe to negate Shakespeare. We know how positive was Goethe's attitude to Shakespeare. It would not have occurred to him to find fault with Shakespeare, because his work led to a satisfying culmination which could be allowed to stand. On the contrary, he found this extraordinarily satisfying.

But the way in which intellectualism developed in his own environment made Goethe depict its existence as something unjustified, whereas he spiritually embraced the political element of what was expressed in the French Revolution. In *Götz von Berlichingen* Goethe is the spiritual revolutionary who denies the spirit in the same way as the French Revolution denies the political element. Goethe turns back in a certain way to something that has once been, though he certainly cannot wish that it should return in its old form. He wants it to develop in a different direction. It is most interesting to observe this mood in Goethe, this mood of revolt against what has come to replace the world of Götz.

So it is extremely interesting to find that Shakespeare has been so deeply grasped by Lessing and by Goethe and that they really followed on from Shakespeare in seeking what they wanted to find through their mood of spiritual revolt. Yet where intellectualism has become particularly deeply entrenched, for instance in Voltaire,[10] it mounts a most virulent attack on Shakespeare. We know that Voltaire called Shakespeare a wild drunkard. All these things have to be taken into account.

Now add something else to the great question which is so important for an understanding of the spiritual revolution which took place in the transition from the fourth to the fifth post-Atlantean period. Add to all this the extraordinary part which Schiller played in this spiritual revolution which in Goethe is expressed in a Goethean way in *Götz von Berlichingen*. In the circle closest of all to Schiller he first met what he had to revolt against. It came out of the most one-sided, unhealthy intellectualism. There was of course as yet no Waldorf school[11] to do battle against one-sided intellectualism. So Schiller could not be sent to the Waldorf school in Wurttemberg but had to go to the *Karlsschule* instead. All the protest which Schiller built up during his youth grew out of his protest against the education he received at the *Karlsschule*. This kind of education—Schiller wrote his drama *Die Räuber* against it—is now universally accepted, and no positive, really productive opposition to it has ever been mounted until the recent foundation of the Waldorf school.

So what is the position of Schiller—who later stood beside Goethe—in all this? He writes *Die Räuber*. It is perfectly obvious to those who can judge such things that in Spiegelberg and the other characters he has portrayed his fellow pupils. Franz Moor himself could not so easily be derived from his schoolmates, but in Franz Moor he has shown in an ahrimanic form[12] everything that his genius can grasp of what lives in his time. If you know how to look at these things, you can see how Schiller does not depict spiritual beings externally, in the way they appear in *Hamlet* or *Macbeth*, but that he allows the ahrimanic principle to work in Franz Moor. And opposite this is the luciferic principle in Karl Moor. In Franz Moor we see a representative of all that Schiller is rebelling against. It is the same world against which Goethe is rebelling in *Götz von Berlichingen*, only Schiller sets about it in a different way. We see this too in the later drama *Kabale und Liebe*.

So you see that here in Central Europe these spirits, Goethe and Schiller, do not depict something in the way Shakespeare does. They do not allow events to lead to something with which one can come to terms. They depict something which is there but which in their opinion ought to have developed quite differently. What they really want does not exist, and what is there on the physical plane is something which they oppose in a spiritual revolution. So we have a strange interplay between what exists on the physical plane and what lives in these spirits.

In a rather bold way I could draw it like this: In Shakespeare the events he depicts carry on in keeping with the way things are on earth

(blue). What he takes in from earlier times, in which the spirit still worked, goes over (red) into a present time which then becomes a factual world evolution.

Then we see in Goethe and Schiller that they had inklings of an

earlier time (red) when the spiritual world was still powerful, in the fourth post-Atlantean period, and that they bring this only as far as their spiritual intentions, whereas they see what is taking place on earth (blue) as being in conflict with it. One thing plays into the other in the human struggle for the spirit. This is why here in Central Europe the question became a purely human one. In the time of Goethe and Schiller a tremendous revolution occurred in the concept of man as a being who stands within a social context. I shall be able to expand on this in the coming lectures.

Let us now look towards the eastern part of Europe. But we cannot look in that direction in the same way. Those who only describe external facts and have no understanding for what lives in the souls of Goethe and Schiller—and also of course many others—may describe these facts very well, but they will fail to include what plays in from a spiritual world—which is certainly also there, although it may be present only in the heads of human beings. In France the battle takes place on the physical earth, in a political revolution. In Germany the battle does not come down as far as the physical plane. It comes down as far as human souls and trembles and vibrates there. But we cannot continue this consideration in the same way with regard to the East, for things are different there. If we want to pursue the matter with regard to the East we need to call on the assistance of Anthroposophy. For what takes place in the souls of Goethe and Schiller, which are, after all, here on the earth—what, in them, blows through earthly souls is, in the East, still in the spiritual world and finds no expression whatsoever down on the earth.

If you want to describe what took place between Goethe's and Schiller's spirits in the physical world—if you want to describe this with regard to the East, then you will have to employ a different view, such as that used in the days of Attila when battles were fought by spirits in the air above the heads of human beings.

What you find being carried out in Europe by Goethe and Schiller—Schiller by writing *Die Räuber* and Goethe by writing *Götz von Berlichingen*—you will find in the East to be taking place as a spiritual fact in the spiritual world above the physical plane. If you want to seek deeds which parallel the writing of *Die Räuber* and the writing of Götz, you will have to seek them among the spiritual beings of the supersensible world. There is no point in searching for them on the physical plane. In a diagram depicting what happens in the East you would have to draw the element in question like a cloud floating above the physical plane, while down below, untouched by it, would be what shows externally on the physical plane.

Now we know that, because we have Hamlet, we can tell how a western human being who had been a pupil of Faust would have behaved, and could have behaved. But there can be no such thing as a Russian Hamlet. Or can there? We could see a Russian Hamlet with our spiritual eyes if we were to imagine the following: Faust lectures at Wittenberg—I mean not the historical Faust but Goethe's Faust who is actually more true than historical fact. Faust lectures at Wittenberg—and Hamlet listens, writing everything down, just as he does even what the ghost says to him about the villains who live in Denmark. He writes everything down in the book and volume of his brain—Shakespeare created a true pupil of Faust out of what he found in the work of Saxo Grammaticus,[13] which depicts things quite differently. Now imagine that an angel being also listened to Faust as he lectured—Hamlet sat on the university bench, Faust stood on the platform, and at the back of the lecture hall an angel listened. And this angel then flew to the East and there brought about what could have taken place as a parallel to the deeds of Hamlet in the West.

I do not believe that it is possible to reach a truly penetrating comprehension of these things by solely taking account of external facts. One cannot ignore the very profound impression made, by these external facts, particularly on the greatest personalities of the time, when what is taking place is something as incisive as the spiritual revolution which took place between the fourth and fifth post-Atlantean periods.

LECTURE TWELVE

Dornach, 25 February 1922

We have been speaking about the tasks facing the leaders of spiritual and cultural life, tasks arising out of the great change that took place in the transition from the fourth to the fifth post-Atlantean period. I endeavoured to describe the forces which emanated from this, such as those which were made manifest in the figure of Faust and the figure of Hamlet. When you consider the essential core of the matter, you find that spiritual leaders such as the poets who created these figures found themselves faced with the task of answering, in poetic form, the question: What will become of the human being when he has to find inner satisfaction of soul from intellectual life alone, living exclusively in abstract thoughts? For obviously the soul's mood as a whole must arise from the impression made on it because it is forced to contemplate, with the help of abstract thoughts alone, all that is most dear to it, and all that is most important for it. All the evolutionary factors we considered yesterday were what Goethe and Schiller had to draw on in their creative work.

We also saw how Goethe and Schiller felt themselves to be ensnared in these evolutionary factors. We saw how both express the feeling that truly great poetic creation cannot be accomplished without some inclination towards the real spiritual world. But the inclination towards the spiritual world which was still characteristic for western cultural development in the eleventh, twelfth, thirteenth centuries was no longer possible in ensuing times. It retreated, you might say, in the face of the stark intellectual view. Yet on the other hand this intellectual view, this living in thoughts, had not yet developed sufficiently to allow access to real, genuine spiritual aspects in the thought life.

What typifies the position of Schiller and Goethe within the cultural evolution of humanity is the fact that their most important creative period falls in an age when the old spirituality has gone, but when it is not yet possible for living spirituality to burgeon out of the new intellectualism. I described a little while ago[1] how that which fills the soul in an intellectual way is actually the corpse of the spiritual life lived by the soul in the world of spirit and soul before birth, or before conception. This corpse must be brought back to life. It must be placed once more within the whole living context of the cosmos.

But this point had not yet been reached at that time, and what Goethe and Schiller were wrestling to achieve, particularly in their most important period, was a mood of soul which could somehow be satisfying during this period of transition, and out of which poetic creation could be achieved.

This shows most clearly and most intensively in the collaboration between Goethe and Schiller. When they met, Goethe had completed a considerable part of *Faust*, namely the Fragment which appeared in 1790 and some additional parts as well. Goethe held back the dungeon scene, even though it was by then already completed. The Fragment has no Prologue in Heaven, but begins with the scene 'I've studied now Philosophy . . .' If we examine this Fragment, and also the parts which Goethe omitted, we find that here Faust stands as a solitary figure wrestling inwardly to find a satisfying mood of soul. He is dissatisfied with stark intellectualism and endeavours to achieve a union with the spiritual world. The Earth-Spirit appears, as in the version now familiar to us. Goethe was certainly striving towards the world of spirit and soul, but what is still entirely lacking, what was still quite foreign to him at that time, was the question of placing Faust within the whole wider cosmic context. There was no Prologue in Heaven. Faust was not yet involved in the battle between God and Satan. This aspect only came to the fore when Schiller encouraged Goethe to continue working on the drama.

Schiller's encouragement inspired him to change Faust's solitary position and place him within the total cosmic context. Encouraged more or less by Schiller, the *Faust* which reappeared in the world in 1808 had been transformed from a drama of personality, which the 1790 version still was, into a drama of the universe. In the Prologue—'The sun makes music as of old, amid the rival spheres of heaven'—in the angels, indeed in the whole spiritual world, and in the opposition with Satan, we see a battle for the figure of Faust which takes place in the spiritual world. In 1790, Faust was concerned only with himself. We see this personality alone; he alone is the focus. But later a tableau of the universe appears before us, in which Faust is included. The powers of good and evil do battle to possess him. Goethe wrote this scene in 1797, placing Faust in a tableau of the universe, after Schiller had demanded of him that he continue work on *Faust*.

As shown in the 'Dedication', Goethe felt somehow estranged from the manner in which he had approached his *Faust* when he was young.

We see also in Schiller what was actually going on in the souls of the most outstanding human beings. He began as a realist. I showed you yesterday how the luciferic and ahrimanic elements confront one another in Karl Moor and Franz Moor. But there is no suggestion of any appearance of the spiritual world in some archetypal figure or other; we see the luciferic and the ahrimanic element simply in the character traits of Karl Moor and Franz Moor. It is quite typical of Schiller to make his point of departure a perfectly realistic element. But when he has completed the plays of his youthful phase, when he has met Goethe, and when he takes up writing again in the nineties, we see that now he is compelled to let the spiritual world play into his poetic creations. It is one of the most interesting facts that Schiller now feels compelled to let the spiritual world play into his poetic figures.

Consider *Wallenstein*. Wallenstein makes his decisions in accordance with his belief in the stars. He acts and forms resolves in accordance with his belief in the stars. So the cosmos plays a role in the figures Schiller creates. The *Wallenstein* drama is comprehensible only when we take into account that Wallenstein feels himself to be filled with the forces which emanate from the starry constellations. At the end of the eighteenth century Schiller felt compelled to return to a contemplation of the stars which was familiar in the sixteenth and seventeenth centuries to those who thought about such things. He felt he could not depict significant events in human life without placing this human life within the cosmos.

Or take *Die Braut von Messina*. He is experimenting. He tries to shape the dramatic action in accordance with the ancient idea of destiny in connection with the wisdom of the stars. It is perfectly obvious that he is trying to do this, for we, too, can experiment with this drama. Take out everything to do with the wisdom of the stars and with destiny, and you will find that in what remains you still have a magnificent drama. Schiller could have written *Die Braut von Messina* without any wisdom of the stars and without any idea of destiny. Yet he included these things. This shows that in his mood of soul he felt the need to place the human being within the cosmos. This quite definitely parallels the situation which led Goethe, on once again taking up work on his *Faust* drama, to place Faust within the tableau of the universe.

Goethe does this pictorially. Angels appear as starry guides. The great tableau of the Prologue in Heaven presents us with a picture of the cosmos. Schiller, who was less pictorial and tended more towards abstraction, felt obliged during the same period to bring into his *Wallenstein* and his *Braut von Messina* something which would hint at the position of the human being within the universe. He even went so far as to include the destiny concept of ancient Greek tragedy.

But look at something else too. Just at the time when he was getting to know Goethe, Schiller, in his own way, adopted the French Revolution's ideas about freedom. I mentioned yesterday that in France the revolution was political, whereas in Central Europe it was spiritual and cultural. I would like to say that this spiritual revolution took on its most intimate character in something Schiller wrote which I have quoted here in all kinds of connections: his *Letters on the Aesthetic Education of Man*.

Schiller asks: How can people achieve an existence which is truly worthy of human beings? Something that might have been called a philosophy of freedom was not yet possible at that time. Schiller answers the question in his own way. He says: A person who follows the course of a logical thought is unfree. Of course he is unfree, because what logic says cannot be developed freely in any way, and so he is subject to the dictates of reasoning. He is not free to say that two times two is six, or perhaps five. On the other hand he is also subject to the dictates of natural laws if his whole organism is given over to the dictates of nature.

So Schiller sees the human being occupying a position between the dictates of reason and the dictates of nature, and he calls the balance between these two conditions the aesthetic condition. The human being shifts the dictates of reason downwards a little into whatever likes and dislikes he may have, thus gaining freedom in a certain sense. And if he can also moderate his urges and instincts—the dictates of nature—raising them up to an extent to which he can rely on them not to debase him to the level of an animal, then they meet up in the middle with the dictates of reason. The dictates of reason take a step down, the dictates of nature take a step up, and they meet in the middle. By acting in accordance with what pleases or displeases him, the human being is in a condition which is subject to neither dictum; he is permitted to do what pleases him, because what pleases him is good by virtue of the fact that at the same time his sensual nature also desires what is good.

This exposition of Schiller's is naturally quite philosophical and abstract. Goethe greatly approved of the thought, but at the same time it was quite clear to him that it could not lead to a solution of the riddle of man. He is sure to have felt deeply for the exceptional spiritual stature of the exposition, for what Schiller achieved in these *Letters on the Aesthetic Education of Man* is indeed one of the best treatises of recent times. Goethe sensed the genius and power of these thoughts. But at the same time he felt that out of such thoughts nothing can come which in any way approaches the being of man. The being of man is too rich to be fathomed by thoughts such as these.

Schiller, if I may say so, felt: Here I am in the intellectual age, but intellectualism makes the human being unfree, for it imposes the dictates of reason. So he sought a way out by means of aesthetic creativity and aesthetic enjoyment. Goethe, though, had a feeling for the infinitely abundant, rich content of human nature. He could not be satisfied with Schiller's view, profound and spiritually powerful though it was. He therefore felt the need to give his own expression to the forces working together in the human being. Goethe, not only by nature, but also because of his whole attitude, was incapable of expressing these things in the form of abstract concepts. Instead, under the influence of the kind of thoughts developed by Schiller, he wrote his fairy-tale of the Green Snake and the Beautiful Lily. Here, about twenty figures appear, all of which have something to do with the forces of the human soul. They work together, not only as the dictates of reason and the dictates of nature but as twenty different impulses which, in the end, depict in the most manifold way something signifying the rich nature of the being of man. We must take note of the fact that Goethe gave up speaking about the being of man in abstract concepts altogether. He felt bound to move away from concepts.

In order to characterize the relationship of Schiller to Goethe in connection with the *Letters on the Aesthetic Education of Man* and the fairy-tale of the Green Snake and the Beautiful Lily, we have to say the following: Goethe wrote the fairy-tale under the immediate influence of Schiller's letters. He wanted to answer the same questions from his point of view and out of his feelings. This can be proved. Indeed I proved it historically long ago and it was seen to make sense.[2] So in order fully to characterize what took place between these two personalities we should have to say: In olden times when, in seeking knowledge, human beings caused beings from the spiritual world to visit them; when they still worked in their laboratories of knowledge in order to penetrate to the mysteries of the universe, and when spiritual beings came into their laboratories—just as the Earth Spirit and many another spirit visit Faust—this was very different from how things are today. In those days people felt themselves to be relatives of those spiritual beings who visited them. They knew, although they were living on the earth and had perforce to make use of the instrument of a physical body, that before birth and after death they were nevertheless beings just like those who visited them. They knew that for earthly life they had sought out an abode which separated them from the spiritual world, but that this spiritual world nevertheless visited them. They knew that they were related to this spiritual world and this gave them an awareness of their own being.

Suppose Schiller had visited Goethe in 1794 or 1795 and had said: Here are my letters on the aesthetic education of man, in which I have endeavoured, out of modern intellectualism, to give people once more the possibility of feeling themselves to be human beings; I have sought the ideas which are necessary in order to speak about the true being of man; these ideas are contained in these letters about aesthetic education. Goethe would have read the letters and on next meeting Schiller he would have been able to say: Well, my friend, this is not bad at all; you have provided human beings once more with a concept of their worth, but this is not really the way to do it; man is a spiritual being, but just as spirits retreat from light, so do they also retreat from concepts, which are nothing other than another form of ordinary daylight; you will have to go about this in a different manner; we shall have to go away from concepts and find something else.

You can find everything I have expressed here, in the form of direct speech, in the correspondence between Goethe and Schiller. It is all there, in hints and intimations. In the process, Goethe wrote his fairy-tale of the Green Snake and the Beautiful Lily, which was to depict how the soul forces work in man. It is Goethe's admission that to speak about man and the being of man it is necessary to rise up to the level of pictures, images. This is the way to Imagination. Goethe was simply pointing out the path to the world of Imaginations. This fairy-tale of the Green Snake and the Beautiful Lily is so very important because it shows that out of his own struggles, and also in his *Faust*, Goethe felt impelled, at a most important moment, to the path towards Imaginations.

To Goethe, the statement that thinking, feeling and will work together in man would have seemed philosophical. He did not say this, but instead he depicted a place where there were three kings, one of gold, one of silver and one of iron. These images signify for him something which cannot be expressed in concepts. We see that

Goethe is on the way to a life of Imagination. This brings us to one of the most profound questions with which Goethe is concerned. He himself did not care to discuss the true profundity of this question with anyone. But we can see how this question concerned him, for it appears in all sorts of places: What is the point of fathoming the being of man by using the kind of thinking to which intellectualism has led? What use would it be? This is a riddle of earthly evolution, a riddle belonging to this epoch, for in this strong form it could only have come into question in this epoch. Sometimes, in all its profundity, it makes its appearance in paradoxical words. For instance in *Faust* we read

The lofty might
Of Science, still
From all men deeply hidden!
Who takes no thought,
To him 'tis brought,
'Tis given unsought, unbidden![3]

This is extraordinarily profound, even if it is only the witch who says it: 'The lofty might of Science, still from all men deeply hidden! Who takes no thought'—in other words to one who does not think—'tis given unsought, unbidden!' However much we think, the lofty might of science remains hidden from us. But if we succeed in not thinking, then it is given unsought, unbidden. So we should develop the might to not think, the skill to not think, in order to achieve not science or knowledge—for this cannot of course be achieved without thinking—but in order to achieve the might of science or knowledge.

Goethe knows that this might of science works in the human being. He knows that it is at work, even in the little child who as yet does not think. What I said in my book *The Spiritual Guidance of Man*[4] was taken very much amiss. On the very first pages I pointed out that if the human being had to fashion all the wisdom-filled things found in the form of the human body by means of his thoughts—consciously using the might which also holds sway in science—then he would reach a ripe old age without ever discovering those delicate formative forces which work with the skill of a sculptor! The might of science is indeed needed in the early years of childhood to transform this brain from a rather formless lump into the sublime structure it has to achieve.

This is a question with which Goethe is profoundly concerned. He of course does not mean merely a dull absence of thinking. But he is quite sure that the might of science can be discovered if we do not destroy our links with it by means of our intellectual thinking. This is even the reason why he makes Mephisto take Faust to the witches' kitchen. Commentaries on these things always distort matters. We fail to know Goethe if we do not link his purpose—in creating a scene like that in the witches' kitchen—with what we sense to be the essence of his own being. Faust is presented with the draught of youth. In one sense he is given a perfectly realistic draught to drink. But the witch says:

See, thus it's done!
Make ten of one,
And two let be,
Make even three,
And rich thou'lt be.
Cast o'er the four!
From five and six
(The witch's tricks)
Make seven and eight,
'Tis finished straight!
And nine is one,
And ten is none.

Now imagine Goethe standing there. If you have a sense for his essential being you cannot but ask: Why is the witch made to declaim this witches' multiplication table? Goethe did not like speaking about these things, but if he were in the right frame of mind he might reply: Well, the lofty might of science, still from all men deeply hidden! Who takes no thought, to him 'tis brought. You see, the power of thought fades when you are told, make ten of one, and two let be, make even three, and rich thou'lt be, and so on. Thinking comes to a standstill! So then you enter into a state of mind in which the lofty might of science can be given to you without any thinking.—Such things are always an aspect of Goethe's *Faust* and indeed of all Goethe's poetic work.

So Goethe was faced with this question, which was for him something exceptionally profound. What was it that Faust lacked, but gained through his sojourn in the witches' kitchen? What did he not have before? If you think of Faust and how he could have been Hamlet's teacher, disgusted by philosophy and jurisprudence, medicine and theology, and turning instead to magic—if you imagine what he is like even in the Easter scene, you will have to admit that he lacks something which Goethe possessed. Goethe never got to the bottom of this. He felt he was like Faust, but he had to say to himself: Yes, all the things with which I have invested Faust are also in me, but there is something else in me as well. Is it something I am permitted to possess? What Faust does not have is imagination, but Goethe did have imagination. Faust gains imagination through the draught of youth which he receives in the witches' kitchen. In a way Goethe answered his own question: What happens when one wants to penetrate to the universal secrets with the help of the imagination? For this was the most outstanding power possessed by Goethe himself.

In his youth he was not at all sure whether looking into the universal secrets with the help of the imagination was anything more than a step into nothingness. This is indeed the Faustian question. For stark intellectuality lives only in mirror images. But once you come to the imagination you are a step nearer to the human being's forces of growth, to the forces which fill the human being. You approach, even though only from a distance, the formative forces which, for instance, shape the brain in childhood. There is then only one more step from the ordinary imagination to the faculty of Imagination! But for Goethe this was the all-important question.

Thus Goethe takes Faust to the witches' kitchen so that he can extricate himself from that confounded capacity of thinking—which may lead to science but does not lead to the might of science—in order that he may be allowed to live in the realm of the imagination. Thenceforward Faust develops his imagination. By means of the draught in the witches' kitchen, Goethe wins for Faust the right to have an imagination. The rejuvenation he experiences is simply a departure from the arid forces he had as, say, a thirty-five year old professor, and a return to his youth where he takes into his soul the youthful formative forces, the forces of growth. Where the imagination flourishes, the youthful formative forces remain alive in the soul.

All this was present as a seed within Goethe, for he wrote the scene in the witches' kitchen as early as about 1788. It was there as a seed, beginning to sprout and demanding a solution. But from Schiller he received a new impulse, for now he was urged on to the path towards the faculty of Imagination. Schiller was at first nowhere near to seeking for the faculty of Imagination. But in *Wallenstein* and in *Die Braut von Messina* he sought the cosmic element.[5] And in *Die Jungfrau von Orleans* he endeavoured to fathom the subconscious forces of the being of man.

The immense profundity of the struggle going on may be seen in the fragment *Demetrius* which Schiller left behind when he died. The dramatic power of this fragment surpasses that of everything else he wrote. In his desk there was also the draft of a play about the Knights of Malta. This, too, if he had succeeded in writing it, would probably have been truly magnificent. The whole principle of the Order of the Knights of Malta—a spiritual order of knighthood resembling that of the Templars—unfolds in their battle against Sultan Suleiman. If Schiller had succeeded in depicting this, he would have been forced to face the question: How will it be possible to bring the vision of the spiritual world down into human creative activity? For this question was indeed alive for him already.

But Schiller dies. Goethe no longer benefits from the stimulus he gave. Later, stimulated by Eckermann—who was less of a spiritual giant than Schiller, if I may put it this way—he finishes *Faust*, working on the second part from about 1824 until his death. Shortly before his death he has the package containing the work sealed. It is a posthumous work. We have considered this second part of *Faust* from many different angles, and have discovered, on the one hand, deeply significant, sublime insights into the manifold mysteries of the spiritual world. Of course we can never understand it entirely if we approach it from this one angle, and we must seek ever higher viewpoints.

But there is another angle too.[6] Goethe felt compelled to complete this poetic work of *Faust*. Let us examine the development of the philosophy of Faust and go back a stage further than we have done so far. One of the stages was the figure of Cyprianus, about whom we have already spoken. Before that, in the ninth century, the legend of Theophilus was written down.[7] Theophilus is once again a kind of Faust of the eighth, or ninth century. He makes a pact with Satan and his fate very much resembles that of Faust.

Consider Theophilus, this Faust of the ninth century, and consider the legendary Faust of the sixteenth century, to whom Goethe refers. The ninth century profoundly condemns the pact with the devil. Eventually Theophilus turns to the Virgin Mary and is saved from all that would have befallen him, had his pact with Satan been fulfilled. The sixteenth century gives the Faust legend a Protestant slant. In the

Theophilus legend, incipient damnation redeemed by the Virgin Mary is described. The sixteenth century protests against this. There is no positive end; the story is told in a manner suitable for Protestantism: Faust makes a pact with the devil and duly falls into his clutches.

First Lessing and then Goethe now protest in their turn. They cannot accept that a character—acting with worldly powers and in the manner of worldly powers—who gives himself over to the power of Satan, entering into a pact with him, must of necessity perish as a consequence of acting out of a thirst for knowledge. Goethe protests against this Protestant conception of the Faust legend. He wants Faust's redemption. He cannot abide by the conclusion of Part One, in which he made concessions and let Faust perish. Faust must be saved. So now Goethe leads us in sublime fashion through the experiences depicted in Part Two. We see how the strong inner being of man asserts itself: 'In this, thy Nothing, may I find my All!'[8] We need only think of words such as these with which a strong and healthy human nature confronts the one who corrupts.

We see Faust experiencing the whole of history up to the time of ancient Greece. He must not be allowed to perish. Goethe makes every effort to arrive at pictures—pictures which, though different in form, are nevertheless taken from the Catholic cultus and Catholic symbolism. If you subtract everything that is achieved out of Goethe's own imaginative life, fuelled as it is by the great riches of the tremendously rich lifetime's experience that was his—if you subtract all this, you find yourself back with the legend of Theophilus in the ninth century. For in the end it is the Queen of Heaven[9] who approaches in all her glory. If you subtract all that specifically belongs to Goethe, you come back to the Theophilus described by the saintly nun Hrosvitha—not identical, of course, but nevertheless something which has not succeeded in an independent approach to the poetic problem but still has to borrow from what has gone before.

We see how a personality as great as Goethe strives to find an entry to the spiritual world. In the fairy-tale of the Green Snake and the Beautiful Lily he is seeking for an Imagination which will make the *human being* comprehensible. In *Faust* he is also seeking for an Imagination, but he cannot achieve an independent Imagination and has to draw on help from Catholic symbolism. Thus his final tableau resembles the clumsy depiction by Hrosvitha in the ninth century—though of course in Goethe's case it is obviously executed by one of the greatest poets.

It is necessary to indicate the intricate paths followed by the spiritual and cultural history of humanity in order to arrive at an understanding of all that is at work in this spiritual history. Only then can we come to realize how the working of karma goes through human history. You need only consider hypothetically that certain things happened which did not actually happen—not in order to correct history in retrospect, but in order to come to an understanding of what is actually there. Imagine that Schiller, who died young, had remained alive. The drama about the Knights of Malta was in his desk and he was in the process of working on *Demetrius*. In collaboration with Goethe the highest spirituality developed in him, living in them both at once. But the thread broke. Look at the second part of *Wilhelm Meister*, look at *Elective Affinities*, and you will see what Goethe was striving for but failed to achieve. Everywhere he was striving to place the human being within a great spiritual context. He was unable to do so, for Schiller had been taken from him.

All this is an expression of the way in which the recent spiritual and cultural evolution of mankind is striving for a certain goal, the goal of seeking the human being in his relationship with the spiritual world. But there are hindrances on every side. Perhaps something like Goethe's *Faust* can be comprehended in all its greatness only when we see what it does not contain, when we see the course on which the whole spiritual evolution of mankind was set. We cannot arrive at an understanding of the spiritual grandeur present in human evolution by merely giving all sorts of explanations, and exclaiming: What an incomparably great masterpiece! We can only reach such an understanding by contemplating the striving of the whole human spirit towards a particular goal of evolution. We are forcefully confronted with this when we consider these things. And then, in the nineteenth century, the thread breaks entirely! The nineteenth century, so splendid in the realm of natural science, sleeps as far as the realm of the spirit is concerned. The most that can be achieved is that the highest wisdom of natural science leads to fault-finding with a creation such as *Faust*.

Goethe needs Schiller, in order to place Faust—whom he first depicted as a personality—within the context of an all-embracing universal tableau. We can sense what Goethe might have made out of the philosophy of Faust if he had not lost Schiller so soon. Yet those who think about these things come along and say that *Faust* is an unfortunate work in which Goethe missed the point entirely. Had he done the thing properly, Faust would have married Gretchen and made an honest woman of her, and then gone on to invent the electro-static machine and the air-pump. Then mankind would have been presented with the proper Faust!

A great aesthete, Friedrich Theodor Vischer,[10] said: *Faust Part Two* is rubbish. So he drafted a plan of what it ought to have been. The result was a kind of improved Eugen Richter out of the nineteenth century, a man of party politics, only a bit more crude than were party men in the nineteenth century. It was not an unimportant person but a very important person—for Friedrich Theodor Vischer was such a one—who stated: The second part of Faust is a piecemeal, fragmented construction of Goethe's old age!

Any connection with a striving for the spirit was lost. The world slept where spirituality was concerned. But out of this very situation the people of today must find their tasks with regard to a new path to the spiritual world. It is of course not possible for us to refer back to:

> The lofty might
> Of Science, still
> From all men deeply hidden!
> Who takes no thought,
> To him 'tis brought,
> 'Tis given unsought, unbidden!

We cannot simply decide to stop thinking, for thinking is a power which came with the fifth post-Atlantean period, and it is a power which must be practised. But it must be developed in a direction which was actually begun by Goethe in his fairy-tale of the Green Snake and the Beautiful Lily. It must be practised in such a way that it leads to Imagination. We must understand that the power of the intellect chases away the spirit, but if the power of the intellect itself can be developed to become the faculty of Imagination, then we can approach the spirit once more. This is what we can learn by considering in a living way what has taken place in the field we have been discussing.

LECTURE THIRTEEN

Dornach, 26 February 1922

The two previous lectures were devoted to considerations intended to show how that tremendous change, which entered into the whole soul constitution of civilized mankind with the fifteenth century—that is, with the transition from the fourth to the fifth post-Atlantean period—continued to have an effect on outstanding personalities. Let me introduce today's lecture with a brief summary of these preceding considerations. I showed how intensely a personality such as Goethe sensed the continuing vibrations of the great change, how he sensed that it was a concrete experience to find intellectual reasoning entering into the human soul. He sensed that it was necessary to come to terms with the intellectual element of the soul and he also had an inkling of the direct intercourse between human beings and the spiritual world which had preceded this intellectual stage. Even though it was no longer as it had been in the days of ancient atavistic clairvoyance, there was nevertheless a kind of looking back to the time when human beings knew that it was only possible for them to find real knowledge if they stepped outside the world of the senses in order to see in some way the spiritual beings who existed behind the sense-perceptible world.

Goethe invested the figure of his Faust with all these things sensed in his soul. We saw how dissatisfied Faust is by stark intellectualism as presented to him in the four academic faculties:

> I've studied now Philosophy
> And Jurisprudence, Medicine,
> And even, alas! Theology,
> From end to end . . .

He is saying in different words: I have loaded my soul with the whole complexity of intellectual science and here I now stand filled with the utmost doubt; that is why I have devoted myself to magic.

Because of dissatisfaction with the intellectual sciences, Goethe invests the Faust figure with a desire to return to intercourse with the spiritual world. This was quite clear in his soul when he was young, and he wanted to express it in the figure of Faust. He chose the Faust figure to represent his own soul struggles. I said that although this is not the case with the historical Faust of the legend, we could nevertheless find in Goethe's depiction of Faust that professor who might have taught at Wittenberg in the sixteenth or even in the seventeenth century, and who had, 'straight or crosswise, wrong or right', led his scholars by the nose 'these ten years long'. This hypothesis allows us to see how in this educational process there was a mixture of the new intellectualism with something pointing back to ancient days when intercourse with the spiritual world and with the spiritual powers of creation was still possible for human beings.

I then asked whether—apart from what is given us in the Faust drama—we might also, in the wider environment, come up against the effects of what someone like Faust could have taught in the fifteenth, sixteenth, seventeenth centuries. And here we hit upon Hamlet, about whom it could be said: The character which Shakespeare created out of Hamlet—who in his turn he had taken from Danish mythology and transformed—could have been a pupil of Faust, one of those very students whom Faust had led by the nose 'these ten years long'. We see Hamlet interacting with the spiritual world. His task is given to him by the spiritual world, but he is constantly prevented from fulfilling it by the qualities he has acquired as a result of his intellectual education. In Hamlet, too, we see the whole transition from the fourth to the fifth post-Atlantean period.

Further, I said that in the whole mood and artistic form of Shakespeare's plays, that is, in the historical plays, we could find in the creativity of the writer of Shakespeare's plays the twilit mood of that time of transition. Then I drew your attention to the way in which Goethe and Schiller in Central Europe had stood in their whole life of soul within the dying vibrations of the transition, yet had lacked, in a certain sense, the will to accept what the intellectual view of the world had since then brought about in the life of human beings. This led them back to Shakespeare, for in his work—*Hamlet*, *Macbeth* and so on—they discovered the capacity to approach the spiritual world; from his vantage point, they could see into the world of spiritual powers which was now hidden from the intellectual viewpoint.

Goethe did this in his *Götz von Berlichingen* by taking the side of the dying echoes of the old time of the fourth post-Atlantean period and by rejecting what had come into being through intellectualism. Schiller, in the dramas of his youth, especially in *Die Räuber*, goes back to that time—not by pointing to the supersensible world, but by endeavouring to be entirely realistic, yet putting into the very words characterizing Karl Moor something which echoes the luciferic element that is also at work in Milton's *Paradise Lost*.[1] In short, despite his realism, we detect a kind of return to a conception of reality which allows the spiritual forces and powers to shine through.

I indicated further that, in the West, Shakespeare was in a position—if I may put it like this—to work artistically in full harmony with his social environment. *Hamlet* is the play most characteristic of Shakespeare. Here the action is everywhere quite close to the spiritual world, as it is also in *Macbeth*. In *King Lear*, for instance, we see how he brings the supersensible world more into the human personality, into an abnormal form of the human personality, the element of madness. Then, in the historical dramas about the kings, he goes over more into realism but, at the same time, we see in these plays a unique depiction of a long drawn-out dramatic evolution influenced everywhere by the forces of destiny, but culminating and coming to an end in the age of Queen Elizabeth.

The thing that is at work in Shakespeare's plays is a retrospective view of older ages leading up to the time in which he lives, a time which is seen to be accepted by him. Everything belonging to older times is depicted artistically in a way which leads to an understanding of the time in which he lives. You could say that Shakespeare portrays the past. But he portrays it in such a way that he places himself in his contemporary western social environment, which he shows to be a time in which things can take the course which they are prone to take. We see a certain satisfaction with regard to what has come about in the external world. The intellectualism of the social order is accepted by the person belonging to the external, physical earthly world, by the social human being, whereas the artistic human being in Shakespeare goes back to earlier times and portrays that aspect of the supersensible world which has created pure intellectualism.

Then we see that in Central Europe this becomes an impossibility. Goethe and Schiller, and before them Lessing, cannot place themselves within the social order in a way which enables them to accept it. They all look back to Shakespeare, but to that Shakespeare who himself went back into the past. They want the past to lead to something different from the present time in which they find themselves. Shakespeare is in a way satisfied with his environment; but they are dissatisfied with theirs.

Out of this mood of spiritual revolution Goethe creates the drama of *Götz von Berlichingen*, and Schiller the dramas of his youth. We see how the external reality of the world is criticized, and how in the artistic realm there is an ebbing and flowing of something that can only be achieved in ideas, something that can only be achieved in the spirit. Therefore we can say: In Goethe and Schiller there is no acceptance of the present time. They have to comfort themselves, so far as external sense-perceptible reality is concerned, with what works down out of the spiritual world. Shakespeare in a way brings the supersensible world down into the sense-perceptible world. Goethe and Schiller can only accept the sense-perceptible world by constantly turning their attention to the spiritual world. In the dramas of Goethe and Schiller we have a working together of the spiritual with the physical—basically, an unresolved disharmony. I then said that if we were to go further eastwards we would find that there is nothing on the earth that is spiritual. The East of Europe has not created anything into which the spirit plays. The East flees from the external working of the world and seeks salvation in the spirit above.

I was able to clothe all this in an Imagination by saying to you: Let us imagine Faust as Hamlet's teacher, a professor in Wittenberg. Hamlet sits at his feet and listens to him, after which he returns to the West and accustoms himself once again to the western way of life. But if we were to seek a being who could have gone to the East, we should have had to look for an angel who had listened to Faust from the spiritual world before going eastwards. Whatever he then did there would not have resembled the deeds and actions of Hamlet on the physical plane but would have taken place above human beings, in the spiritual world.

Yesterday, I then described how, out of this mood, at the time when he was making the acquaintance of Schiller, Goethe felt impelled to bring the being of man closer to the spiritual world. He could not do this theoretically, in the way Schiller, the philosopher, was able to do in his aesthetic letters, but instead he was urged to enter the realm of Imagination and write the fairy-tale of the Green Snake and the Beautiful Lily. Then Schiller felt the urge to bring the external reality of human life closer to the spirit—I might say experimentally—in *Wallenstein*, by letting a belief in the stars hold sway like a force of destiny over the personality of Wallenstein, and in *Die Braut von Messina* by letting a destiny run its course virtually entwined with a belief in the stars. These personalities were impelled ever and again to turn back to the time when human beings still had direct intercourse with the spiritual world.

Further, I said that Goethe and Schiller lived at a time when it was not yet possible to find a new entry into the spiritual world from out of a modern soul constitution. Schiller in particular, with his philosophical bent, had he lived longer and finished the drama about the Knights of Malta, would have come to an understanding of how, in an order like this, or like that of the Templars, the spiritual worlds worked together with the deeds of human beings. But it was not granted to Schiller to give the world the finished drama about the Knights of Malta, for he died too soon. Goethe, on the other hand, was unable to advance to a real grasp of the spiritual world, so he turned back. We have to say that Goethe went back to Catholic symbolism, the Catholic cultus, the cultus of the image, though he did so in an essentially metamorphosed form. We cannot help but be reminded of the good nun Hrosvitha's legend of Theophilus[2] from the ninth century, when Goethe in his turn allows Faust to be redeemed in the midst of a Christianizing tableau. Although his genius lets him present it in a magnificently grand and artistic manner, we cannot but be reminded, in 'The Eternal Feminine bears us aloft', of the Virgin Mary elevating the ninth-century Theophilus.

An understanding of these things gives us deep insight into the struggle within intellectualism, the struggle in intellectualism which causes human beings to experience inwardly the thought-corpse of what man is before descending through birth—or, rather, through conception—into his physical life on earth. The thoughts which live in us are nothing but corpses of the spirit unless we make them fruitful through the knowledge given by spiritual science. Whatever we are, spiritually, up to the moment when earthly life begins, dies as it enters our body, and we bear its corpse within us. It is our earthly power of thought, the power of thought of our ordinary consciousness.

How can something that is dead in the spiritual sense be brought back to life? This was the great question which lived in the souls of Goethe and Schiller. They do not bring it to expression philosophically but they sense it within their feeling life. And they compose their works accordingly. They have the feeling: Something is dead if we remain within the realm of the intellect alone; we must bring it to life. It is this feeling which makes them struggle to return to a belief in the stars and to all sorts of other things, in order to bring a spiritual element into what they are trying to depict. It is necessary for us to be aware of how the course of world evolution is made manifest in such outstanding personalities, how it streams into their souls and becomes the stuff of their struggles. We cannot comprehend our present time unless we see that what this present time must strive for—a new achievement of the spiritual world—is the very problem which was of such concern for Goethe and Schiller.

What happened as a result of the great transition which took place in the fifteenth century was something of which absolutely no account is taken in ordinary history. It was, that the human being acquired an entirely different attitude towards himself. But we must not endeavour to capture this in theoretical concepts. We must endeavour to trace it in what human beings sensed; we must find out how it went through a preparation and how it later ran its course after the great change had been fulfilled in its essential spiritual force.

There are pointers to these things at crucial points in cultural evolution. See how this comes towards us in Wolfram von Eschenbach's *Parzival*.[3] You all know the story. You know how crucial it was for the whole of Parzival's development that he first of all received instruction from a kind of teacher as to how he was to go through the world without asking too many questions. As a representative of that older world order which still saw human beings as having direct intercourse with the spiritual world, Gurnemanz says to Parzival: Do not ask questions, for questioning comes from the intellect, and the spiritual world flees from the intellect; if you want to approach the spiritual world you must not ask questions.

But times have changed and the transition begins to take place. It is announced in advance: Even though Parzival goes back several more centuries, into the seventh or eighth century, all this was nevertheless experienced in advance in the Grail temple. Here, in a way, the institutions of the future are already installed, and one of them is that questions must be asked. The essential point is that with the transition from the fourth to the fifth post-Atlantean period the situation of the human being changes. Previously it was inappropriate to ask questions because conditions held sway about which Goethe speaks so paradoxically:

The lofty might
Of Science, still
From all men deeply hidden!
Who takes no thought,
To him 'tis brought,
'Tis given unsought, unbidden!

In those times it was right not to ask questions, for that would have driven away the spirits! But in the age of the intellect the spiritual world has to be rediscovered through the intellect and not by damping down the processes of thought. The opposite must now come into play; questions must be asked. As early as Parzival we find a portrayal of the great change which brings it about in the fifth post-Atlantean period that the longing for the spiritual world now has to be born out of the human being in the form of questions to be formulated.

But there is also something else, something very remarkable, which comes to meet us in Parzival. I should like to describe it as follows. The languages which exist today are far removed from their origins, for they have developed as time has gone on. When we speak today—as I have so often shown—the various combinations of sounds no longer remind us of whatever these combinations of sounds denote. We now have to acquire a more delicate sense for language in order to experience in it all the things that it signifies. This was not the case where the original languages of the human race were concerned. In those days it was known that the combination of sounds itself contained whatever was experienced in connection with the thing depicted by those sounds. Nowadays poets seek to imitate this. Think, for instance, of 'Und es wallet und siedet und brauset und zischt'.[4] Poetic language has here imitated something of what the poet wants us to see externally. But this is mere derived imitation. In olden times every single sound in language was felt to have the most intimate connection with what was happening all around. Today only some local dialects can lay claim to giving us some sense for the connection between external reality and the words spoken in dialect. However, language is still very close to our soul—it is a special element in our soul.

It is another consequence of the transition from the fourth to the fifth post-Atlantean period that this has become deposited as something very deeply sensed within the human soul, again a fact which is left out of account by both philology and history. The fact that in the fourth post-Atlantean period human beings lived more within their language and that in the fifth post-Atlantean period this is no longer the case, brings about a different attitude by human beings towards the world. You can understand that human beings with their ego are linked quite differently to what is going on around them if, in using language, they go along with all the rushing of waves, the thundering and lightning, and whatever else is happening out there. This becomes ever more detached as the transition from the fourth to the fifth post-Atlantean period progresses. The ego becomes more inward, and language together with the ego also becomes more inward, but at the same time less meaningful as regards external matters. Such things are most certainly not perceived by the knowledge of today, which has become so intellectual. There is hardly any concern to describe such things. But if what is taking place in mankind is to be correctly understood, they will have to be described.

Imagine what can come into being. Imagine vividly to yourselves, here the fourth post-Atlantean period, and here the fifth. The transition is of course gradual, but for the sake of explanation I shall have to talk in extremes. In the fourth post-Atlantean period you have here the things of the world (green). The human being with his words, depicted within him, here in red, is still connected with the things. You could say he 'lives over' into the things through the medium of his words. In the fifth post-Atlantean period the human being possesses his words within his soul, separated off from the world.

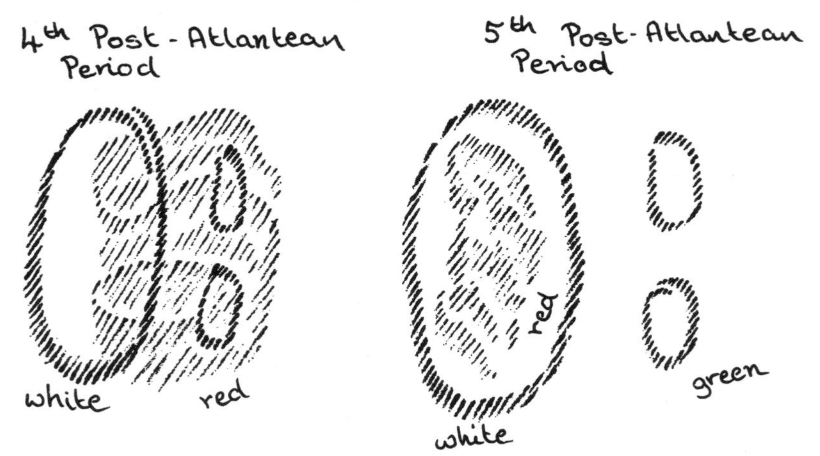

Imagine this clearly, even almost in grotesque detail. Looking at the human being here in the fourth post-Atlantean period, you might say of him that he still lives with the things. The things he does in the outside world will proceed to take place in accordance with his words. If you see one of these human beings performing a deed, and if at the same time you hear how he describes the deed, there is a harmony between the two. Just as his words are in harmony with external things, so are his deeds in harmony with the words he speaks. But if a human being in the fifth post-Atlantean period speaks, you can no longer detect that his words resound in what he does. What connection with the deed can you find today in the words: I have chopped wood! In what is taking place out there in the activity of chopping we can no longer sense in any way a connection with the movement of the chopper. As a result, the connection with the sounds of the words gradually disappears; they cease to be in harmony with what is going on outside. We no longer find any connection between the two. So then, if someone listens pedantically to the words and actually does what lies in the words, the situation is quite different. Someone might say: I bake mice. But if someone were actually to bake mice, this would seem grotesque and would not be understood.

This was sensed, and so it was said: People ought to consider what they actually have in their soul in conjunction with what they do externally; the relationship between the two would be like an owl looking in a mirror! If someone were to do exactly what the words say, it would be like holding up a mirror to an owl. Out of this, in the second half of the fourteenth century, *Till Eulenspiegel* arose.[5] The owl's mirror is held up in front of mankind. It is not Till Eulenspiegel who has to look in the mirror. But because Till Eulenspiegel takes literally what people say with their dry, abstract words, they suddenly see themselves, whereas normally they do not see themselves at all. It is a mirror for the owls because they can really see themselves in it.

Night has fallen. In past times, human beings could see into the spiritual world. And the activity of their words was in harmony with the world. Human beings were eagles. But now they have become owls. The world of the soul has become a bird of the night. In the strange world depicted by Till Eulenspiegel, a mirror is held up before the owl.

This is quite a feasible way of regarding what appears in the spiritual world. Things do have their hidden reasons. If we fail to take note of the spiritual background, we also fail to understand history, and with it the chief factor in humanity today. It is especially important to depart from the usual external characterization of everything. Look in any dictionary and see what absurd explanations are given for Eulenspiegel! He cannot be understood without entering into the whole process of cultural and spiritual life. The important thing in spiritual science is to actually discover the spirit in things, not in a way that entails a conceptual knowledge of a few spiritual beings who exist outside the sense-perceptible world, but in a way which leads us to an ability to see reality with spiritual eyes.

The change which took place, between the time when human beings felt themselves to be close to the spiritual world and the later time when they felt as though they had been expelled from that world, can be seen in other areas too. Try to develop a sense for the profound impulse which runs through something like the Parzival epic. See how Parzival's mother dresses him in a simpleton's clothes because she does not want him to grow up into the world which represents the new world. She wants him to remain in the old world. But then he grows up from the sense-perceptible world into the world of the spirit.

The seventeenth century also possesses a kind of Parzival, a comical Parzival, in which everything is steeped in comedy. In the intellectualistic age, if one is honest, one cannot immediately muster the serious attitude of soul which prevails in Parzival. But the seventeenth century too, after the great change had taken place, had its own depiction of a character who has to set out into the world, lose himself in it, finally ending-up in solitude and finding the salvation of his soul. This is Christoffel von Grimmelshausen's *Simplicissimus*.[6] Look at the whole process of the story. Of course you must take the whole tone into account, on the one hand the pure, perhaps holy mood of Parzival, and on the other the picaresque, comical mood. Consider Simplicissimus, the son of well-to-do peasants in the Spessart region. In the Thirty Years' War their house is burnt down. The son has to flee, and finds his way to a hermit in the forest who teaches him all kinds of things, but who then dies. So here he is, abandoned in the world and having to set off on his travels. He becomes immersed in all the events and blows of fate offered by the Thirty Years' War. He arrives at the court of the governor of Hanau. Externally he has learnt nothing, externally he is a pure simpleton; yet he is an inwardly mature person for all that. But because externally he is a pure simpleton the governor of Hanau says to himself: This is a simpleton, he knows nothing; he is Simplicissimus, as naive as can be. What shall I train him to be? I shall train him to be my court fool.

But now the external and the internal human being are drawn apart. The ego has become independent in respect of the external human being. It is just this that is shown in *Simplicissimus*. The external human being in the external world, trained to be the court fool, is the one who is considered by all and sundry to be a fool. But in his inner being Simplicissimus in his turn considers all those who take him for a fool to be fools themselves. For although he has not learnt a thing, he is nevertheless far cleverer than all those who have made him into a fool. He brings out of himself the other intellectuality, the intellectuality that comes from the spirit, whereas what comes to meet him from outside is the intellectuality that comes from reasoning alone. So the intellectualists take him for a fool, and the fool brings his intellectualism from the spiritual world and holds those who take him for a fool to be fools themselves. Then he is taken prisoner by some Croats, after which he roams about the world undergoing many adventures, until finally he ends up once more at the hermitage where he settles down to live for the salvation of his soul.

The similarity between Simplicissimus and Parzival has been recognized, but the crucial thing is the difference in mood. What in Parzival's case was still steeped in the mind-soul has now risen up into the consciousness soul. Now caustic wit is at work, for the comical can only have its origin in caustic wit. If you have a feel for this change of mood, you will be able to discover—especially in works which have a broader base than that of a single individuality—what was going on in human evolution. And Christoffel von Grimmelshausen did indeed secrete in *Simplicissimus* the whole mood, the whole habit of thought of his time. Similarly you can in a way find the people as a whole composing stories, and gathering together all the things which the soul, in the guise of an owl, can see in the mirror, and which become all the tall tales found in *Till Eulenspiegel*.

It would be a good thing, once in a while, to go in more detail into all these things, not only in order to characterize the various interconnections. I can only give you isolated examples. To say everything that could be said I should have to speak for years. But this is not really what matters. What is crucial is to come closer to a more spiritual conception of these things. We have to learn to know how things which are presented to us purely externally are also connected with the spirit. So we may say: That tremendous change which took place in the transition from the fourth to the fifth post-Atlantean period can be seen everywhere, vibrating through the cultural and spiritual evolution of mankind. As soon as you step back a bit from this turning-point of time, you come to see how all the different phenomena point to the magnititude of the change.

Only by taking the interconnections into account is it possible to understand what lies hidden in the figures brought by spiritual and cultural life out of the past and into the present. Take Lohengrin, the son of Parzival. What does it mean that Elsa is forbidden to ask after his name and origin? People simply accept this. Not enough deep thought is given to the question as to why she is forbidden to ask, for usually there are two sides to everything. Certainly this could also be described differently, but one important aspect may be stated as follows: Lohengrin is an ambassador of the Grail; he is Parzival's son. Now what actually is the Grail community? Those who knew the mystery of the Grail did not look on the Grail temple as a place solely for the chosen knights of the Grail. They saw that all those who were pure in heart and Christian in the true sense went to the Grail while they slept—while they were between sleeping and waking. The Grail was seen as the place where all truly Christian souls gathered while they slept at night. There was a desire to be apart from the earth. So those who were the rulers of the Grail also had to be apart from earthly life. Lohengrin, the son of Parzival, was one of these. Those who desired to work in accordance with the Grail impulse had to feel themselves entirely within the spiritual world. They had to feel that they belonged entirely to the spiritual world and certainly not at all to the earthly world. In a certain sense you could say that they had to drink the draught of forgetfulness.

Lohengrin is sent down from the Grail castle. He unites with Elsa of Brabant, that is with the people of Brabant. In the train of Heinrich I he sets out to fight the Hungarians. In other words, at the instigation of the Grail he carries out important impulses of world history. The strength he has from the Grail temple enables him to do this. When we go back to the fourth post-Atlantean period we find that all these things are different. In those days spiritual impulses played their part together with external impulses that could be comprehended by the intellect. This is hardly noticeable in the way history is told today.

We speak quite rightly today of meditative formulae, simple sentences which work in the human being's consciousness through their very simplicity. How many people today understand what is meant when history tells us that those required to take part in the Crusades—they took place in the fourth post-Atlantean period—were provided with the meditative formula 'God wills it' and that this formula worked on them with spiritual force. 'God wills it' was a kind of social meditation. Keep a look out for such things in history; you will find many! You will find the origins of the old mottos. You will discover how the ancient titled families set out on conquering expeditions under such mottos, thus working with spiritual means, with spiritual weapons. The most significant spiritual weapons of all were used by knights of the Grail, such as Lohengrin. But he was only able to use them if he was not met with recollections of his external origins, his external name, his external family. He had to transport himself into a realm in which he could be entirely devoted to the spiritual world and in which his intercourse with the external world was limited to what he perceived with his senses, devoid of any memories. He had to accomplish his deeds under the influence of the draught of forgetfulness. He was not allowed to be reminded. His soul was not permitted to remember: This is my name and I am a scion of this or that family. So this is why Elsa of Brabant is not allowed to question him. When she does, he is forced to remember. The effect on his deeds is the same as if his sword had been smashed.

If we go back beyond the time when everything became intellectual, so that people also clothed what had gone before in intellectual concepts, imagining that everything had always been as they knew it—if we go back beyond what belongs to the age of the intellect, we find the spiritual realm working everywhere in the social realm. People took the spiritual element into account, for instance, in that they took moral matters just as much into account as physical medicines.

In the age of the intellect, in which all people belong only to the intellect, whatever would they think if they found that moral elements, too, were available at the chemist's! Yet we need only go back a few centuries prior to the great change. Read *Der Arme Heinrich* by Hartmann von Aue,[7] who was a contemporary of Wolfram von Eschenbach. Before you stands a knight, a rich knight, who has turned away from God, who in his soul has lost his links with the spiritual world, and who thus experiences this moment of atheism which has come over him as a physical illness, a kind of leprosy. Everyone avoids him. No physician can cure him. Then he meets a clever doctor in Salerno who tells him that no physical medicine can do him any good. His only hope of a cure lies in finding a pure virgin who is prepared to be slain for his sake. The blood of a pure virgin can cure him of his illness. He sells all his possessions and lives alone on a smallholding cared for by the tenant farmer. The farmer has a daughter. She falls in love with the leprous knight, discovers what it is that alone can cure him, and decides to die for him. He goes with her to the doctor in Salerno. But then he starts to pity her, preferring to keep his illness rather than accept her sacrifice. But even her willingness to make the sacrifice is enough. Gradually he is healed.

We see how the spirit works into cultural life, we see how moral impulses heal and were regarded as healing influences. Today the only interpretation is: Ah, well, perhaps it was a coincidence, or maybe it is just a tale. Whatever we think of individual incidents, we cannot but point out that, during the time which preceded the fifteenth century, soul could work on soul much more strongly than was the case later; what a soul thought and felt and willed worked on other souls. The social separation between one human being and another is a phenomenon of intellectualism. The more intellectualism flourishes and the less an effort is made to find what can work against it—namely the spiritual element—the more will this intellectualism divide one individuality from another.

This had to come about; individualism is necessary. But social life must be found out of individualism. Otherwise, in the 'social age' all people will do is be unsociable and cry out for Socialism. The main reason for the cry for Socialism is that people are unsocial in the depths of their soul. We must take note of the social element as it comes towards us in works such as Hartmann von Aue's *Der arme Heinrich*. It makes its appearance in cultural works in which it can be sensed quite clearly through the mood. See how different is the mood in *Der arme Heinrich*. You cannot call it sentimental, for sentimentality only arose later when people found an unnatural escape from intellectualism. The mood is in a way pious; it is a mood of spirituality. To be honest about the same matters in a later age you have to fall back on the element of comedy. You have to tell your story as Christoffel von Grimmelshausen did in *Simplicissimus*, or as the people as a whole did in *Till Eulenspiegel*.

This sense of having been thrown out of the world is found everywhere, not only in poetic works arising out of the folk element. Wherever it appears, you find that what is being depicted is a new attitude of the human being towards himself. From an entirely new standpoint he asks: What am I, if I am a human being? This vibrates through everything. So from the new intellectual standpoint the question is asked over and over again: What is the human being? In earlier times people turned to the spiritual world. They truly sought what Faust later seeks in vain. They turned to the spiritual world when they wanted to know: What actually is the human being? They knew that outside this physical life on earth the human being is a spirit. So if he wants to discover his true being, which lives in him also in physical, earthly life, then he will have to turn to the spiritual world.

Yet more and more human beings are failing to do this very thing.

In *Faust* Goethe still hints: If I want to know the spirit, I must turn to the spiritual world. But it does not work. The Earth Spirit appears, but Faust cannot recognize it with his ordinary knowledge. The Earth Spirit says to him: 'Thou'rt like the Spirit which thou comprehendest, not me!'[8] Faust has to turn away and speak to Wagner. In Wagner he then sees the spirit which he comprehends. Faust, 'image of the Godhead', cannot comprehend the Earth Spirit. So Goethe still lived in an age which strove to find the being of man out of the spiritual world. You see what came once Goethe had died. Once again people wanted to know what the human being is, this time on the basis of intellectualism. Follow the thread: People cannot turn to the spiritual world in order to discover what the human being is. In themselves, equally, they fail to find the answer, for language has meanwhile become an owl in the soul. So they turned to those who depicted olden times at least in an external fashion. What do we find in the nineteenth century?[9] In 1836 Jeremias Gotthelf: *Bauernspiegel*; in 1839 Immermann: *Oberhof*, *Die drei Mühlen*, *Schwarzwälder Bauerngeschichten*; George Sand: *La Petite Fadette*; in 1847 Grigorovich: *Unhappy Anthony*; in 1847-51 Turgeniev: *Sportsman's Sketches*.

We have here the longing to find in simple people the answer to the question: What is the human being? In olden times you turned to the spiritual world. Now you turned to the peasant. During the course of two decades the whole world develops a longing to write village stories in order to study the human being. Because people cannot recognize themselves, at best looking in the mirror as if they are owls, they turn to simple folk instead. What they can prove in every detail, from Jeremias Gotthelf to Turgeniev, is that everything is striving to get to know the *human being*. In all these village stories, in all these simple tales, the unconscious endeavour is to achieve a knowledge of man. From this kind of viewpoint spiritual and cultural life can become comprehensible.

This is what I wanted to show you in these three lectures, in order to illustrate the transition from the fourth to the fifth post-Atlantean period. It is not enough to describe this transition with a few abstract concepts—which is what was naturally done at first. Our task is to illumine the whole of reality with the light of the spirit through Anthroposophy. These lectures have been an example of this.

LECTURE FOURTEEN

Dornach, 19 March 1922

Many reasons have led us to consider how the age of intellectualism—which we have often also called the age of the fifth post-Atlantean culture—begins in the transition from the thirteenth to the fourteenth and fifteenth centuries. In this age, human beings come to regard the intellect as the dominant factor in all their endeavours. We have often spoken of the way in which this intellectualism has come to develop in the various realms of inner life. Everything that is characteristic for human evolution has its more inward aspect through which it lives more expressly in people's feelings, in their views, in their dominant will impulses, and so on. At the same time it also has an outward aspect which manifests in the conditions and circumstances which arise historically in human evolution. In this connection it has to be said that the most significant expression of the intellectualistic age so far has been the French Revolution, that great world-wide movement of the end of the eighteenth century.

For long ages before it took place, much in the life of mankind pointed to ways of striving for the very kind of social community which then came to be expressed so tumultuously in this French Revolution. And since then much has remained of the French Revolution, flickering into life here or there in one form or another in the external social conditions of mankind. Only consider that the French Revolution, in the way it manifested at the end of the eighteenth century, could not have been possible previously. For prior to those days human beings did not seek full satisfaction on this earth with regard to everything they were striving for.

You must understand that before the time of the French Revolution there was never a period in the history of mankind when people expected everything human beings can strive for, in thought, feeling and will, to find an external expression in earthly life. In the times which preceded the French Revolution, people knew that the earth can never provide for every single requirement of man's spirit, soul and body. Human beings always felt that they had links with the spiritual world and they expected this spiritual world to satisfy whatever requirements cannot be satisfied by the earthly world.

However, long before the French Revolution expressed itself in such a tumultuous fashion there were endeavours in many realms of the civilized world to introduce a social order which would allow as many human needs as possible to be satisfied here on earth. The fundamental character of the French Revolution itself was the endeavour to found a social environment which would be an expression here on earth of human thinking, feeling and willing. This is essentially what intellectualism seeks, too.

The realm of intellectualism is earthly existence. Intellectualism wants to satisfy everything that is present in the sense-perceptible physical world. So it wants to organize the social situation here on earth to be an expression of the intellectual element. The endeavour to create in social conditions something which man can strive for here on earth, even goes to the extent of the worship of the goddess of reason—which means, of course, the goddess of the intellect. So we can say: In very ancient times human beings ordered their lives according to the impulses which came to them from initiates and mystery pupils; through them they took into their social order the divine spiritual world itself. Then social conditions moved on to those of, let us say, Egypt, when the social order took in what the kings learnt from the priests about the will of human evolution as it was expressed, for instance, in the stars. Later still, in older Roman times, the times of the Roman kings, the endeavour was made to bring about social conditions based on research into the spiritual world. The meeting of Numa Pompilius with the nymph Egeria is an expression of this.[1] More and more out of this interweaving of the spiritual with the earthly, social realm came the requirement: Everything on earth is to be arranged in such a way as to be a direct expression of the intellect.

To express this in a diagram you would have to draw a downward curve. The French Revolution comes at the lowest point (see sketch), and from here onwards things had to start moving upwards once more. This upward movement was indeed immediately attempted as a reaction to the French Revolution. Read Schiller's *Letters on the Aesthetic Education of Man*. There we can see quite clearly, for instance, how he was stimulated by what was expressed in the French Revolution in an external way to seek a new connection to the spiritual world within man's inner being. For Schiller the question arose: If it is impossible to create a perfect social order here on earth, how can human beings achieve satisfaction with regard to their thinking, feeling and will? How can they achieve freedom here on this earth?

And Schiller answered this question by saying: If human beings

live logically, in accordance with the dictates of reason, they are servants of the dictates of reason and not free beings. If they follow their physical urges and instincts alone, then in turn they are following the dictates of nature and are unfree. He then came to say: The human being is actually only free when he is working artistically or when he is enjoying something artistic. The achievement of freedom in the world can only come about when the human being works artistically or enjoys art. Artistic activity balances what is otherwise either a dictate of reason or a dictate of nature, as Schiller puts it. Living in the artistic realm, the human being feels the compulsion of thoughts less with regard to an artistic object than he does in the case of logical research. Similarly, what comes to him from the object of art through his senses is not a sensual urge. The sensual urge is ennobled by the spiritual seeing of something artistic. So inasmuch as a human being is capable of working artistically he is also capable of unfolding freedom within earthly existence.

Schiller seeks to answer the question: How can man as a social being achieve freedom? And the conclusion he reaches is that the human being can only achieve freedom if he is a being who is receptive to art. He cannot achieve freedom by being devoted to the dictates of reason or the dictates of nature.

At the time when Schiller was writing his *Letters on the Aesthetic Education of Man* this came to expression in a wonderful way in the interaction between Goethe and Schiller. This is shown in the way Schiller perceived how Goethe was rewriting his *Wilhelm Meister* at that time. Schiller was full of enthusiasm for this way of writing and for this depiction of inner freedom, because Goethe as an artist was a creative spirit—not in his intellect but in the freedom of his thoughts—yet one who, on the other hand, still remained within a sensual experience of art. Schiller sensed this. He felt that Goethe in his artistic activity was as free as is a child at play. We see how Schiller is enthused by a free human artistic activity which is reminiscent of a child at play. His enthusiasm led him to say in one of his letters to Goethe: The artist is the true human being; in comparison even the best philosopher is a mere caricature.[2] But his enthusiasm also led him to say: The human being is only truly human when he is at play, and he only plays when he is truly human.[3] Frivolous or merely entertaining play is not meant, but artistic activity and artistic enjoyment. The human being dwells within artistic experience, which means that the human being becomes truly free: This is what Schiller is saying.

At the point where the line starts to curve upwards from what had been—with regard to a social order—the goal of the French Revolution, towards something for which human beings have to wrestle inwardly and which cannot be given to them by institutions of the state; at this point, what price was the human being willing to pay for this social freedom? He was prepared to pay the price that it could not be given to him through logical thinking and that it could not be given to him through ordinary physical life, but that he could receive it only in the exclusive activity of artistic experience.

These feelings were indeed engraved within the best spirits of that age, in Schiller in a theoretical form, and in Goethe too, who actually practised this life in freedom. Let us look at the characters Goethe created out of life itself in order to reveal genuine humanity, the true human being. Look at *Wilhelm Meister*. Wilhelm Meister is a personality through whom Goethe wanted to depict the true human being. Yet seen from an overall view of life he is actually a layabout. He is not a person who is seriously searching for a world view which includes the human soul. Neither is he someone who can manage to hold down a job in external life. He loiters his way through life. This is because the ideal of freedom striven for in the work of Goethe and Schiller could only be achieved by people who had removed themselves from a thoughtful and hard-working way of life. It is almost as if Schiller and Goethe had wanted to point to the illusion of the French Revolution, to the illusory belief that something external, like the state, might make human beings free. They wanted to point out that human beings can only wrestle for this freedom within themselves.

Herein lies the great contrast between Central Europe and Latin western Europe. Latin western Europe believed in an absolute sense in the power of the state, and it still believes in it today. In Central Europe, on the other hand, came the reaction that the human ideal can only be found within. But the price for this would have to be the inability to stand squarely in life. Someone like Wilhelm Meister had to disentangle himself from life.

So we see that at the first attempt it proved impossible to find full humanity within a true human being. Naturally, if everybody is to become an artist so that, as Schiller put it, society can become entirely aesthetic, this may be all very well, but such an aesthetic society would not be very good at coping with life. I cannot imagine, for instance—let me be really down to earth for a moment—how in such an aesthetic society the sewers will be kept clear. Neither can I imagine how in this aesthetic society certain things will be achieved which ought to be achieved in accordance with strictly logical concepts. The ideal of freedom shone before mankind, but human beings were unable to strive for this ideal of freedom when they stood fully within life. It became necessary to search once more for an impetus upwards to the supersensible world, but now this had to be done consciously, just as in former times there had been an atavistic downward impetus. A new upward impetus into the spiritual world had to be sought. It was necessary to hold on to the ideal of freedom but, at the same time, the upward impetus had to be sought. First it had to be made possible to secure freedom for human activity, for active involvement in life. It seemed to me that the only possible way was that described in my *Philosophy of Freedom*.[4]

If human beings can achieve the impetus to rise up to an inner constitution of soul which enables them to find moral impulses in pure thoughts, in the way I have just described, then they will be free beings even though they remain squarely within full, everyday life. This is why I had to introduce into my *Philosophy of Freedom* the concept of moral tact, which is otherwise not found in moralizing sermons, the concept of acting as a matter of course out of moral tact, by means of which moral impulses can flow over into habitual deeds.

Consider the role played by tact, by moral good taste, in my *Philosophy of Freedom*. There you see that in an aesthetic society true human freedom is only applied to the feelings, whereas it actually ought to be brought also into the will, that is, into every aspect of the human being. A human being who has achieved a soul constitution in which pure thoughts can live in his will as moral impulses, can enter fully into life, however burdensome it may be, and he will be able to stand in this life as a free being in so far as this life calls for actions, deeds.

Furthermore, with regard to the dictates of reasoning, that is, the grasping of the world in thoughts, a way also had to be sought of finding what it is that guarantees freedom for the human being, independence from external compulsions. This could only come about through anthroposophical spiritual science. Learning to find their way into what can be experienced in spirit with regard to cosmic mysteries and cosmic secrets, human beings live in thoughts with their humanness into a closeness with the inner spirit of the world. Through freedom they achieve knowledge of the spirit.

What is going on here is best demonstrated by the way in which people, with regard to this, are still strenuously resisting becoming free. This is a point of view from which opposition to Anthroposophy can very well be understood. Human beings do not want freedom in the spiritual realm. They want to be compelled, led, guided by something. And since every individual is free either to recognize or deny the spirit, most deny it and choose instead something which they are not free either to recognize or deny.

No free decision is required to recognize or deny thunder and lightning, or the combination of oxygen or hydrogen in some laboratory process. But human beings are free to recognize that angeloi and archangeloi exist. Or they can deny their existence. But those who truly possess an impulse for freedom come through this very impulse for freedom to the recognition of the spiritual in thinking. In Schiller's *Letters on the Aesthetic Education of Man*, in the whole of Goethe's creative work, the achievement of human freedom through inner effort and struggle was first attempted. But this can only be achieved if we recognize that to our freedom in the realm of artistic experience must be added a free experience in the realm of thinking and a free experience in the realm of the will. These are things which must be properly developed.

Schiller simply took what the age of the intellect had to offer. In Schiller's time art still arose out of this intellectualism. Within this, Schiller still discovered human freedom. But what intellectualism has to offer in the realm of thinking is something unfree, something which is subject to the dictates of logic. And Schiller failed to recognize the possibility that freedom might also hold sway here, just as little as it might hold sway in deeds, in ordinary, hard life. What we have had to achieve through the introduction of anthroposophical spiritual science is the recognition that freedom can also be recognized in the realm of thinking and in the realm of the will. Schiller and Goethe recognized freedom solely in the realm of feeling.

But the path to a full recognition of human freedom can only be trodden if human beings are able to achieve an inner vision of the connection between the spiritual realm they can experience in their soul, and the realm of nature. So long as two abstract concepts, nature and spirit, are seen by human beings as being mutually exclusive, it will not be possible for them to progress to a proper conception of the freedom I have been describing. But even those who do not work their way towards life in the spiritual world, by means of meditation, concentration exercises and so on, can certainly experience something, if they are willing to recognize, simply with their healthy common sense, what has been found through Imagination, Inspiration and Intuition. Simply by reading in books or hearing in lectures what is brought to the fore in the world through Imagination—and provided they remain alert—people will soon need to approach these revelations from the spiritual world in a way that differs from their approach, say, to a book on physics or chemistry, or on botany or zoology, even though this different approach can just as much take a course which follows ordinary healthy common sense.

Without developing any great inner activity it is possible to absorb everything written today in a book about botany or zoology. But it is not possible to absorb what I have described, for instance, in my book *Occult Science*, without inner energy and activity such as that needed also for ordinary healthy common sense. Everything in this book can be understood, and those who maintain that it is incomprehensible are simply unwilling to think actively; they want to absorb it as passively as they absorb a film in the cinema. In the cinema there is certainly no need to think very much, and it is in this manner that people today want to absorb everything. What they find in the laboratory can also be absorbed in this way. But what is said in my book *Occult Science* cannot by absorbed in this way. Occasionally some professorial souls do attempt to absorb it in this way. In consequence, they then make the suggestion that whose who perceive such things ought to be examined in psychological laboratories, as they are called today. This suggestion is just as clever as requiring someone who solves mathematical problems to be examined in order to ascertain whether he is capable of solving mathematical problems. To such a person it is said: If you want to find out whether these mathematical problems have been solved correctly, you will have to learn how to solve them, and then you will be able to check. Only if he were stupid would he retort: No, I don't want to learn how to check on the solutions; I shall go to a psychological laboratory in order to find out whether they are correct! These are the kinds of demands made today by some professorial souls, and their words are taken up by all sorts of 'generals'[5] and repeated parrot-fashion with evil intent. Such demands are foolish and stupid, but this does not prevent them from being made with the greatest aplomb.

But those who enter with inner activity into what comes from Imagination will certainly find that something bears fruit in their soul. It is not insignificant for the soul when an effort is made to understand something that has been discovered through Imagination. For instance, it is extremely difficult today to make medicines effective for the treatment of illnesses. But someone who has made the effort to understand something given through Imagination will have reactivated his vital forces to such an extent that medicines will once more be effective for him—provided they are the right ones—because his organism will no longer reject them.

It is stupidly suggested nowadays that anthroposophical medicines are supposed to heal people spiritually through hypnosis and the power of suggestion. You can read this in all manner of magazines which refer to remarks I have made on my lecture tours in recent months. But this is, in the first instance, not the point. The point is that today's medical knowledge needs to be advanced positively through spiritual knowledge. Of course it is not possible to heal somebody by inoculating him with an idea. Yet spiritual life, taken quite concretely, does have significance for the effectiveness of medicines. If a person endeavours to understand something given through Imagination, he makes his organism more receptive to medicines—provided they are the ones needed for his illness—than is the organism of a person who remains in the thought structure of today's external intellectualism, that is, of today's materialism.

Mankind needs to take in what can be given by Imagination, if only for the reason that the human physical body will otherwise succumb more and more to a condition in which it cannot be healed if it falls ill. Healing always requires assistance from the element of spirit and soul. All the processes of nature find expression not only in what takes place on the sense-perceptible plane. These processes on the physical plane are everywhere steeped in the element of spirit and soul. To make a sense-perceptible substance effective in the human organism you need the element of soul and spirit. The whole process of human evolution requires that the soul make-up of human beings should once more be filled with what can be grasped by soul and spirit.

It is true to say that amongst human beings there is certainly much longing for soul and spirit. But for the most part this longing remains within the unconscious or the subconscious realm. Meanwhile, what remains within human consciousness is no more than a mere remnant of intellectualism, and this rejects—indeed resists—anything spiritual. The manner in which spiritual things are resisted is sometimes quite grotesque. Before a performance of eurythmy I usually explain that eurythmy is based on an actual, visible language. Just as the language of sounds develops out of the way the physical organism is arranged, so it is with the visible language that is eurythmy. Just as—sound for sound—all vowels, all consonants struggle to be born out of the experience of the human organism, so in eurythmy is sound for sound gathered together, resulting in genuine language. You would think that on being introduced to eurythmy people might endeavour to find their way into the fundamental impulse which tells us that eurythmy is a language, is speech.

Of course it is perhaps not immediately obvious as to what is meant. But with serious intent it is not too difficult to find one's way quite quickly into what is meant. The other day someone read something really funny in a review of a eurythmy performance. The critic pointed out that the impossible nature of this eurythmy performance was revealed in the fact that the performers first gave a rendering of some earnest, serious items, and that they followed these with some humorous pieces. The extraordinary thing, said this witty critic, was that the humorous items were depicted with the same gestures as the serious ones. That is the extent to which he understood the matter. He thought that humorous things ought to be shown with sound gestures that are different from those used to depict serious matters. Now if you take seriously the fact that eurythmy is a visible language, then what this critic says would amount to saying that any language ought to have one set of sounds for serious things and another for humorous things! In other words, somebody reciting something in German or French would use sounds such as I or U, or whatever, but that on coming to a humorous item they would use other sounds.

I don't know how many people noticed what utter nonsense this critic was writing in one of Germany's foremost newspapers; but this is what he was saying in reality. This shows that in such heads every capacity for thinking clearly has ceased; they are entirely unable to think any more.

This is the final consequence of intellectualism, which is gaining ground today in all realms of life. People begin by allowing their thoughts to become the dead inner content of their soul. How rigid, how dead are most thoughts which are produced these days; how little inner mobility they have, how much are they parroted from models created earlier on! There are extraordinarily few original thoughts in our present age. But something that has died—and thoughts today are mostly thoughts that have died—does not remain constantly in the same state. Look at a corpse after three days, after five years or after forty years. It goes on dying, it goes on decomposing. If somebody states that a eurythmy performance is impossible because it uses the same gestures for humorous and for serious items, this is a thought that is decomposing. And if this is not noticed it is simply because people are incapable of schooling their common sense by means of inspired truths such as those arising out of Anthroposophy. If people school their common sense by means of inspired truths, even if they do not undertake any spiritual development, then they acquire a delicate sense for the living truth, and for what is healthy and unhealthy in human thinking and in human endeavour. And then—if you will pardon my saying so—statements such as the one I have just quoted begin to stink. People acquire the capacity to smell the stench of such decomposing thoughts. This capacity, this sense of smell, is for the most part lacking amongst our contemporaries. Most of them do not notice these things, they read them without taking them in.

It is certainly necessary to look very thoroughly into what mankind needs. For human beings definitely need that freedom of thinking in their soul constitution which can only become possible if they raise themselves to a position in which they can take in spiritual truths. Without this we come to that decline of culture which is clearly to be seen all around us today. Healthy judgment, the right immediate impression—these are things which mankind has for the most part already lost. They must not be allowed to get lost, but only if human beings can press through to an acceptance of spiritual things will they not be lost.

We must pay attention to the fact that human beings can find in

Anthroposophy a meaningful content for their lives if they turn with their healthy common sense to what can be won through Imagination, Inspiration and Intuition. By opening themselves to what can be discovered, for example, through Imagination, they can recapture that inner vitality which will make them receptive to medicines. Or, it may be that they will also become free personalities who are not prone to succumb to all sorts of public suggestions.

By entering in a living way into the truths revealed by Inspiration, they can gain a sure sense for what is true or false. And they can become skilful in putting this sure sense into practice in the social sphere. For instance, how few people today are able to listen properly! They are incapable of listening, for they react immediately with their own opinion. This capacity to listen to other human beings can be developed most beautifully by entering in a living way into the truths given by Inspiration.

And by entering in a living way into the truths given by Intuition, human beings can develop to a high degree something else which they need in their lives: a certain capacity to let go of their own selves, a kind of selflessness. Entering in a living way into the truths given by Imagination, Inspiration and Intuition, this gives human beings a meaningful content for their lives.

Of course, it is easier to say that people can gain a content for their lives out of what Ralph Waldo Trine[6] promises. It is easier to say they need only read the content of something in order to gain a content for their lives, whereas it is more difficult to obtain a content for life in an anthroposophical way. For along this path you have to work; you have to work in order to enter in a living way into what research reveals through Imagination, Inspiration and Intuition. But then it becomes a content for life which unites intensely with the personality and with the whole human being. This secure life content is what is given by what wishes to enter the world as Anthroposophy.

NOTES

Lecture One

1 *Yesterday I spoke about initiation science*: See lecture of 31 December 1921 in Rudolf Steiner, *The Rediscovery of Spiritual Reality in Nature and in Man*. English text available in typescript only.

2 This lecture was given during the 1921/22 Christmas course for teachers: Rudolf Steiner, *Soul Economy and Waldorf Education*, Rudolf Steiner Press London and Anthroposophic Press New York, 1986.

3 *luciferic or ahrimanic*: Regarding luciferic and ahrimanic beings, see the chapter 'Man and the Evolution of the World' in Rudolf Steiner, *Occult Science—An Outline*, Rudolf Steiner Press, London 1979.

4 *which starts with Augustine*: Aurelius Augustinus 354-430, Bishop of Hippo in North Africa.

5 *Bismarck made a remarkable statement*: in a speech on 9 May 1884, 'I recognize unconditionally the right to work and will defend this so long as I occupy my present position. In doing so, I stand, not on the soil of socialism but on the soil of the Prussian constitution.' Quoted in Gide and Rist *Geschichte der volkswirtschaftlichen Lehrmeinungen, Jena 1921.*

6 *Maximilien Francois Marie Isidore de Robespierre*, 1758-1794. From 1793 a leading member of the Committee of Public Safety. Guillotined in 1794.

Lecture Two

1 *Vladimir Soloviev*, 1853-1900. The quotation in German is from *Die geistigen Grundlagen des Lebens*, Part One (The Spiritual Foundations of Life), Selected Works translated by H Köhler, Stuttgart 1922.

2 See Lecture One, Note 4.

Lecture Three

1 Rudolf Steiner, *Occult Science—An Outline*. For the post-

Atlantean cultural periods see the chapter 'Man and the Evolution of the World'.

2 *a cosmosophy, a philosophy, a religion*: See also Rudolf Steiner, *Philosophy, Cosmology and Religion*, Anthroposophic Press, New York 1984, and Rudolf Steiner's own reports of these lectures in *Cosmology, Religion and Philosophy*, Anthroposophic Press, New York 1984.

3 *Johannes Scotus Erigena* c.810-877. Irish philosopher and theologian, one of the most notable thinkers of the Carolingian Middle Ages. His principal work *De divisione naturae* was burnt by Pope Honorius in Paris in 1225.

Lecture Four

1 *some recent historical events*: There are numerous gaps in the shorthand report of this lecture. The conclusion has been omitted. It deals with contemporary questions and covers virtually the same ground as Lecture One (Soloviev, Bismarck, Robespierre).

2 *about which the Apostle Paul taught*: For example 1 Corinthians, 15.

3 *Waldorf school*: The Free Waldorf School, Stuttgart, was founded by Rudolf Steiner in 1919. The education of the children was to be in harmony with the knowledge of the human being as revealed by anthroposophical spiritual science.

4 Herbert Spencer, 1820-1903. *Education: Intellectual, Moral and Physical*, 1861.

5 Vladimir Soloviev: See Lecture Two, Note 1.

6 Adolf von Harnack, 1851-1930. Theologian and historian.

7 *Council of Nicaea*: 19 June 325. Establishment of the creed of identity of Son (Jesus Christ) and Father.

Lecture Five

1 Rudolf Steiner *Knowledge of the Higher Worlds. How is it achieved*? Rudolf Steiner Press, London 1985.

2 *Vienna lecture cycle*: Rudolf Steiner, *The Inner Nature of Man and the Life between Death and New Birth*, Anthroposophical Publishing Company, London 1959.

Lecture Six

1 *Today*: In his introduction to this lecture (contained in GA 255), Rudolf Steiner spoke words of appreciation for the way in which Albert Steffen had reported in the journal *Das Goetheanum* on a lecture denigrating Anthroposophy.
2 Thales of Miletus, c.640-545 BC.
3 Rudolf Steiner, *Riddles of Philosophy*, Anthroposophic Press, New York 1973.
4 *early church fathers*: For instance, St Justin Martyr, *Apologia I*, 46.
5 Rudolf Steiner, *Christianity as Mystical Fact*, Rudolf Steiner Press, London 1972.

Lecture Seven

1 *Order of the Knights of Malta*: In 1798 Napoleon seized and occupied Malta on his way to Egypt.
2 *a public lecture*: See the lecture of 2 November 1921 in Rudolf Steiner, *Anthroposophie und Wissenschaft*, Dornach GA 75 (not yet published).
3 Rudolf Steiner *Theosophy*, Anthroposophic Press, New York 1986.
4 David Lloyd George, 1863-1945. British Prime Minister from 1916 to 1922.
5 *In the nineties*: On 16 February 1894 Ernst Haeckel celebrated his sixtieth birthday. Rudolf Steiner was one of the invited guests. Bismarck, much admired by Haeckel, was also present. He had been forced to resign his office in 1890.

Lecture Nine

1 Philo of Alexandria, c.20 BC—c.40 AD. Jewish philosopher and theologian.
2 Pedro Calderón de la Barca, 1600-1681. Greatest Spanish dramatist. The drama about Cyprianus, *El mágico prodigioso* (The Miracle-working Magician) was written in 1637. The story was taken from a late version of an old tale in the *Golden Legend*. It is set in Antioch at the time of the Roman Emperor Decius.
3 Gotthold Ephraim Lessing, 1729-1781. German dramatist, critic and writer on aesthetics; one of the great seminal minds in German literature.

Lecture Ten

1 *The fairy-tale of the Green Snake and the Beautiful Lily*: Floris Books, Edinburgh 1979. See, for instance, Rudolf Steiner, *The Portal of Initiation & The Character of Goethe's Spirit as Shown in the Fairy Story (incl. a translation of the Fairy Story by Thomas Carlyle*, Rudolf Steiner Press, New Jersey 1961.
2 '*The sun makes music*': Johann Wolfgang von Goethe, *Faust, Part One*, 'Prologue in Heaven'. The English versions of the quotations from *Faust* are taken from the translation by Bayard Taylor, with the exception of these lines from the 'Prologue in Heaven', which are translated by Shelley. (Tr.)
3 *first Mystery Drama: The Portal of Initiation. A Rosicrucian Mystery* through Rudolf Steiner, transl. Ruth and Hans Pusch, Steiner Book Centre, Toronto, 1973.
4 *his scientific writings*: Rudolf Steiner *Goethes Naturwissenschaftliche Schriften, mit Einleitungen, Fussnoten und Erläuterungen im Text* (Goethe's Natural Scientific Writings) in Kürschners *Deutsche National-Litteratur*. On the intermaxillary bone see Volume 1.
5 *Paul's words*: Galatians 2, 20.
6 '*Stand on free soil*': *Faust*: Part Two, Act 5, Great Outer Court of the Palace.
7 Karl Julius Schröer, 1825-1900. On his booklet *Goethe und die Liebe* (Goethe and Love) see Rudolf Steiner's collected essays 1921-1925 in *Der Goetheanumgedanke inmitten der Kulturkrisis der Gegenwart*, p.111. GA 36.
8 '*He who would study*': *Faust* Part One. The Study.
9 *essay by Ruedorffer*: J.J. Ruedorffer, *Die drei Krisen. Eine Untersuchung über den gegenwärtigen politischen Weltzustand* (The Three Crises. A consideration of the present state of world politics.) Stuttgart/Berlin 1920.
10 Franz Overbeck, 1837-1905.

Lecture Eleven

1 *post-Atlantean periods*: See Lecture Three, Note 1.
2 *Calderón*: See Lecture Nine, Note 2.
3 *Faust belongs to the sixteenth century*: The first mention of Faust appeared in 1506. In 1587 the first *Faustbuch*, a popular chapbook, was published in Frankfurt-am-Main.

4 *'Philosophy and Jurisprudence'*: *Faust* Part One. The Study.
5 Johann Gottfried Herder, 1744-1803. Called Kant's system 'a kingdom of never-ending whims, blind alleys, fancies, chimeras and vacant expressions.'
6 Emil Du Bois-Reymond, 1818-1896: In 'Goethe und kein Ende' (No end to Goethe), address of 15 October 1882 in *Reden* (Speeches), Leipzig 1886.
7 William Shakespeare, 1564-1616. *Hamlet* is one of his later plays.
8 *'book and volume of his brain'*: *Hamlet*, Act One, Scene 5.
9 *'what one has in black and white'*: *Faust Part One*, The Study.
10 Francois-Marie Arouet Voltaire, 1694-1778. One of the greatest French authors.
11 *Waldorf school*: See Lecture Four, Note 3.
12 *in an ahrimanic form*: See Lecture One, Note 3.
13 Saxo Grammaticus, d.1204. Danish historian who wrote the *Gesta Danorum*.

Lecture Twelve

1 *a little while ago*: For instance see Rudolf Steiner *The Bridge Between Universal Spirituality and the Physical Constitution of Man*, Anthroposophic Press, New York 1958, lecture of 19 December 1920; and Rudolf Steiner, *The Shaping of the Human Form out of Cosmic and Earthly Forces*, lecture of 26 November 1920. English text available in typescript only.
2 *was seen to make sense*: See Rudolf Steiner, *Goethe as Founder of a New Science of Aesthetics*, Anthroposophical Publishing Company, London 1922; and Rudolf Steiner, *Goethe's Secret Revelation* and *The Riddle of Faust*, Rudolf Steiner Publishing Co., London 1933.
3 *'The lofty might'*: *Faust*, Part One, Witches' Kitchen. The quotation 'See, thus it's done!' is also from this scene.
4 Rudolf Steiner, *The Spiritual Guidance of Man*, Anthroposophic Press, New York, 1983.
5 *he sought the cosmic element*: See Rudolf Steiner, *Schiller und die Gegenwart* (Schiller and the Present Time), Dornach 1955, lecture in Berlin on 4 May 1905.
6 *another angle too*: See Rudolf Steiner *Geisteswissenschaftliche Erläuterungen zu Goethes Faust*, (Goethe's *Faust* Illumined by Spiritual Science), Dornach 1967, GA 272 and 273.

7 *legend of Theophilus*: This legend, of Greek origin, came to the West some time around the tenth century and was recounted both in prose and in verse in almost every known language. Hrosvitha, the poetess from Lower Saxony, a nun in Gandersheim, told the story in Latin verse.
8 *'In this, thy Nothing'*: Faust to Mephisto in *Faust* Part Two, A Gloomy Gallery.
9 *the Queen of Heaven: Faust* Part Two, last scene.
10 Friedrich Theodor Vischer (1807-1887), philosopher and aesthete. In 1862 he wrote a satire *Faust. Der Tragödie dritter Teil* (The Tragedy of Faust, Part Three).

Lecture Thirteen

1 John Milton, 1608-1674. English poet and puritan politician. His epic poem *Paradise Lost* was finished by 1665.
2 *legend of Theophilus*: See Lecture Twelve, Note 7.
3 Wolfram von Eschenbach, c.1170-1220. One of the greatest medieval German poets. *Parzival* was probably written between 1200 and 1210.
4 'Und es wallet...': 'And it bubbles and seethes, and it hisses and roars', *Der Taucher* by Friedrich von Schiller, translated by E. Bulwer Lytton in *The Poems and Ballads of Schiller*, Leipzig 1844.
5 Till Eulenspiegel, a popular German peasant jester, was supposed to have died in Mölln in 1350. The first extant text of the chapbook in High German chronicling his escapades was published in 1515. The name 'Eulenspiegel' means, literally, 'owl's mirror'. (Tr.)
6 Christoffel von Grimmelshausen, d.1676. German writer. *Simplicissimus*, published in 1669, is said to be the greatest German novel of the seventeenth century.
7 Hartmann von Aue, c.1170-1213. Middle High German poet. *Der arme Heinrich* (Poor Henry).
8 *'Thou'rt like the spirit'*: *Faust* Part One. The Study.
9 *in the nineteenth century*: Jeremias Gotthelf (A. Bitzius), 1797-1854; Karl Immermann, 1796-1840; George Sand (A.A.L. Dupin-Dudevant), 1804-1876; D.W. Grigorovich, 1818-1883; I.S. Turgeniev, 1818-1883.

Lecture Fourteen

1 Numa Pompilius, 715-672 BC. Roman King. By tradition, the nymph Egeria was his wife and adviser.
2 *a mere caricature*: Letter to Goethe of 7 January 1795.
3 Schiller, *On the Aesthetic Education of Man*, Letter 15.
4 Rudolf Steiner, *The Philosophy of Freedom*, Rudolf Steiner Press, London 1988.
5 '*Generals*': This is a reference to speeches given by General von Gleich.
6 Ralph Waldo Trine, 1866-1958. *In Tune with the Infinite*, London 1915.

Typescripts are available at the Library, Rudolf Steiner House, 35 Park Road, London NW1.